Table of Contents

6

9

Chapter 1: Mastering the CryEngine Ecosystem

1.1 Deep Dive into Advanced CryEngine Features

In this section, we will explore the advanced features and capabilities of CryEngine, a powerful game engine known for its stunning graphics, dynamic environments, and flexible toolset. Whether you're a seasoned developer or just getting started, understanding these features will enable you to create more immersive and engaging games.

Understanding CryEngine's Rendering Pipeline

CryEngine boasts a sophisticated rendering pipeline that allows for realistic lighting, shadows, and materials. The engine leverages physically-based rendering (PBR) to simulate how light interacts with objects, resulting in visually stunning scenes. To take full advantage of this, developers can create custom shaders and materials to achieve unique visual styles.

```
-- Sample shader code
function customShader()
    -- Define shader properties and calculations here
end
```

Advanced Physics Simulations

CryEngine provides robust physics simulations that go beyond basic collision detection. Developers can create complex interactions such as realistic destruction, fluid dynamics, and interactive elements. This level of realism enhances gameplay and immersion.

```
// Example code for creating realistic destruction
void onExplosion(Vector3 position, float radius) {
    // Implement destruction effects here
}
```

Leveraging CryEngine's AI Capabilities

CryEngine's AI system allows for the creation of intelligent and adaptive NPCs. Developers can craft complex AI behaviors, implement dynamic NPC interactions, and design advanced pathfinding and navigation systems. This is crucial for creating lifelike and challenging opponents.

```
// AI behavior script
void patrol() {
    // Define patrol behavior here
}

void attackPlayer() {
    // Implement NPC's attack strategy
}
```

Multiplayer Integration and Networking

CryEngine supports seamless multiplayer experiences, including both peer-to-peer and dedicated server setups. Developers can implement advanced networking concepts for scalability, security, and cheat prevention. Synchronizing complex multiplayer elements ensures a smooth and enjoyable online gaming experience.

```
# Network synchronization code
def synchronizePlayerPosition(playerID, newPosition):
    # Synchronize player positions across clients
```

Extensive Asset Management

Efficient asset management is crucial in game development. CryEngine provides tools for organizing, importing, and optimizing assets efficiently. With the right asset management strategies, you can streamline your workflow and enhance productivity.

```
# Command line asset import
cryengine import models/character.fbx
```

Staying Updated with CryEngine

CryEngine continuously evolves with updates and new releases. Staying informed about these changes is vital for taking advantage of the latest features and improvements. Engaging with the CryEngine community and following official resources will help you keep your projects up-to-date.

In this section, we have scratched the surface of the advanced features of CryEngine. As you delve deeper into its capabilities, you'll unlock new possibilities for your game development projects. Whether you're interested in rendering, physics, AI, multiplayer, asset management, or staying current with updates, mastering CryEngine is a rewarding journey.

1.2 Efficient Workflow Strategies for Experienced Developers

In this section, we will explore various workflow strategies tailored for experienced developers using CryEngine. These strategies are designed to maximize efficiency, collaboration, and productivity throughout the game development process.

Version Control and Collaboration

Experienced developers understand the importance of version control systems such as Git or SVN. These tools allow teams to work collaboratively on CryEngine projects while maintaining a history of changes. By utilizing branching, merging, and pull requests, developers can manage code and assets seamlessly.

```
# Git command for creating a new branch
git checkout -b feature/new-feature
```

Modular Asset Creation

Efficiency in asset creation is paramount. Experienced developers often adopt a modular approach, creating reusable assets and components. This approach not only saves time but also ensures consistency in design and reduces redundancy.

```
// Modular asset creation
- Characters
    - CharacterBase.cryasset
    - CharacterArmor.cryasset
    - CharacterWeapon.cryasset
```

Scripting and Automation

Automation is a key aspect of efficient workflows. Developers can use scripting languages like Python or Lua to automate repetitive tasks in CryEngine. This includes asset importing, level generation, and even build processes.

```
# Python script for batch asset import
import os

def import_assets(directory):
    for filename in os.listdir(directory):
        if filename.endswith(".fbx"):
            cryengine.import_asset(os.path.join(directory, filename))
```

Continuous Integration (CI) and Testing

Experienced developers integrate CI systems into their workflow to automatically build, test, and deploy their CryEngine projects. CI ensures that changes do not introduce errors or regressions, maintaining project stability.

```
# Example CI configuration (using Jenkins)
stages:
    - build
    - test
    - deploy
```

```
# Run automated tests
test:
    script:
        - cryengine run-tests
```

Documentation and Knowledge Sharing

Documentation is a vital component of efficient workflows. Experienced developers maintain detailed documentation for code, assets, and project-specific guidelines. This knowledge sharing empowers team members and facilitates onboarding for new developers.

Character Animation Pipeline

```
1. Import character model.
2. Rig character with the provided skeleton.
3. Animate using the animation rig.
4. Export animations to CryEngine-friendly format.
```

Task Management and Agile Methodologies

Experienced developers often employ Agile methodologies like Scrum or Kanban to manage tasks and prioritize work effectively. Task boards, sprint planning, and daily stand-ups are common practices to keep development on track.

```
**Sprint 1 (2 weeks)**
- Task 1: Implement character movement
- Task 2: Create level prototype
- Task 3: Rig and animate main character
```

Profiling and Optimization

Efficiency includes optimizing for performance. Profiling tools in CryEngine help identify bottlenecks and performance issues. Experienced developers regularly profile their projects and optimize critical sections of code and assets.

```
// CryEngine profiling output
Frame Time: 16.7ms (60 FPS)
- Rendering: 7.5ms
- Physics: 2.2ms
- AI: 1.8ms
- Scripting: 0.5ms
```

Continuous Learning

Experienced developers recognize the ever-evolving nature of game development. They allocate time for continuous learning, whether through online courses, tutorials, or attending industry events. Staying up-to-date with CryEngine's new features and industry trends is essential.

In conclusion, efficient workflow strategies are essential for experienced developers using CryEngine. These strategies encompass version control, modular asset creation, scripting and automation, continuous integration, documentation, task management, profiling, and continuous learning. By implementing these practices, developers can streamline their processes and deliver high-quality games more effectively.

1.3 Customizing the CryEngine Environment

In this section, we will delve into the customization options available within the CryEngine environment. Customizing CryEngine can greatly enhance your workflow, making it more tailored to your specific needs and preferences.

Configuring Editor Layouts

CryEngine's editor allows for the customization of layouts, enabling you to arrange panels, views, and tabs according to your workflow. Experienced developers often create custom layouts that cater to their specific tasks, whether it's level design, scripting, or asset management.

```
**Custom Layout: Level Design**
- Primary View: 3D viewport
- Panels: Entity Outliner, Terrain Editor
- Tabs: Objects, Layers
```

Creating Custom Tools and Plugins

CryEngine supports the development of custom tools and plugins using C++ and Lua scripting. These tools can automate tasks, provide specialized functionality, or integrate external software. By creating custom tools, you can streamline repetitive actions.

```
-- Lua script to automate asset import
function importAssets(directory)
    -- Implement asset import logic here
end
```

Customizing Keybindings and Shortcuts

Experienced developers often customize keybindings and shortcuts to match their preferred workflow. CryEngine allows you to map specific actions to keyboard shortcuts, mouse buttons, or even game controllers. This personalization can significantly speed up your work in the editor.

```
// Custom keybindings
- F1: Toggle Console
- Ctrl+Shift+S: Save Level
- Alt+RightClick: Pan Viewport
```

Asset Pipeline Customization

CryEngine provides options to customize the asset pipeline, including importing and exporting settings. You can define how assets are processed, compressed, and optimized during import and export. This level of control ensures that assets are tailored to your project's requirements.

```
# Asset pipeline configuration
- Model Import Settings:
  - Compression: Lossless
```

```
- LODs: Auto-generate
- Normal Maps: Generate
```

Theme and Visual Customization

CryEngine allows you to customize the visual theme of the editor. You can choose from various themes or create your own color schemes to make the interface more visually appealing or to fit a specific project's aesthetics.

```
// Editor theme customization
- Theme: Dark Mode
- Custom Colors: Blue accent
```

Extending CryEngine with Plugins

CryEngine's extensibility goes beyond custom tools. You can also create and integrate custom plugins that add new features or functionality to the engine. This flexibility enables you to adapt CryEngine to the unique requirements of your project.

```
// Example C++ plugin code
class MyCustomPlugin : public CryHooksModule
{
public:
    // Implement custom functionality here
};
```

Scripting Customization

Lua and C++ scripting in CryEngine provide extensive opportunities for customization. You can script custom behaviors, systems, or even automate complex tasks within the engine. This level of control is invaluable for creating unique gameplay experiences.

```
// C++ script for custom gameplay mechanics
void customAbility(PlayerEntity player) {
    // Implement custom ability logic here
}
```

UI Customization

CryEngine's user interface (UI) is also customizable. You can create custom UI elements, menus, and HUD components to match the style and requirements of your game. This ensures that the in-game UI aligns with your project's vision.

```
<!-- Custom HUD element -->
<UIElement type="image" name="customHUD" position="10,10" size="100,100" texture="hud_custom.png" />
```

Sharing Customization with the Community

One of the advantages of customizing CryEngine is the potential to share your creations with the community. Whether it's custom tools, themes, or plugins, contributing to the

CryEngine ecosystem can be a rewarding way to give back and collaborate with fellow developers.

In conclusion, customizing the CryEngine environment offers experienced developers a powerful set of tools to tailor the engine to their specific needs. From configuring editor layouts to creating custom tools, keybindings, and plugins, customization options abound. By personalizing CryEngine, you can optimize your workflow and make game development more efficient and enjoyable.

1.4 Advanced Asset Management and Organization

Efficient asset management is a fundamental aspect of successful game development with CryEngine. In this section, we will explore advanced techniques and best practices for organizing and managing assets within your CryEngine projects.

Asset Naming Conventions

Establishing clear and consistent naming conventions for assets is essential. Experienced developers often adopt naming conventions that indicate the asset type, category, and purpose. This makes it easier to locate and identify assets, reducing confusion and streamlining the development process.

```
**Naming Convention Example:**
- Characters
  - CH_MainCharacter.cryasset
- Weapons
  - WP_Rifle.cryasset
- Textures
  - TX_WoodTexture.cryasset
```

Folder Structure Design

Creating a well-structured folder hierarchy is crucial for keeping your project organized. Developers often design folder structures that reflect the game's components and systems. This approach simplifies asset management and ensures that assets are intuitively grouped.

```
**Folder Structure Example:**
- Assets
  - Characters
  - Environments
  - Weapons
  - Textures
```

Metadata and Tags

CryEngine allows developers to assign metadata and tags to assets. Metadata can include descriptions, authors, and usage notes. Tags help categorize assets based on various criteria, making it easier to filter and search for specific assets within the project.

```
// Asset metadata and tags
- Asset Name: CH_MainCharacter.cryasset
- Author: John Smith
- Tags: Character, Player, Hero
```

Dependency Tracking

Managing dependencies between assets is crucial. CryEngine offers tools for tracking asset dependencies to ensure that changes to one asset do not break others. This is particularly important for complex projects with many interconnected assets.

```
// Asset dependency tracking
- MainCharacter.cryasset depends on Skeleton.cryasset
- Rifle.cryasset depends on Ammo.cryasset
```

Version Control Integration

Integrating your CryEngine project with version control systems like Git or SVN is a standard practice. Version control helps track changes to assets, allows for collaboration, and provides a history of asset modifications. It ensures that you can always revert to previous versions if needed.

```
# Git command to commit asset changes
git commit -m "Updated character textures"
```

Asset Documentation

Maintaining documentation for assets is valuable. Developers often create documentation that includes asset descriptions, usage instructions, and reference images. This documentation aids both the asset creators and other team members working with the assets.

```
**Texture Documentation**
- Asset Name: TX_WoodTexture.cryasset
- Description: High-resolution wood texture for environmental assets.
- Usage: Apply to 3D models, terrain materials, or props.
- Reference: [Link to texture reference image]
```

Asset Optimization

Optimizing assets is crucial for performance. CryEngine provides options for asset optimization, including LOD (Level of Detail) generation, texture compression, and mesh simplification. Experienced developers carefully balance asset quality and performance.

```
// Asset optimization settings
- LODs: Automatically generate LODs
- Texture Compression: DXT5
- Mesh Simplification: Enabled
```

Asset Backups and Versioning

Creating regular backups of important assets is a best practice. Additionally, implementing asset versioning within your project ensures that you can access previous iterations of assets in case of errors or design changes.

```
**Asset Versioning:**
- Character Model (v1)
- Character Model (v2, current)
- Character Model (v3, experimental)
```

Asset Collaboration Workflow

Collaborating on assets requires a well-defined workflow. Developers often establish procedures for asset creation, review, and integration. Clear communication and role assignments help maintain asset quality and consistency.

In conclusion, advanced asset management and organization are critical for a successful CryEngine project. Establishing naming conventions, creating a logical folder structure, using metadata and tags, tracking dependencies, integrating version control, documenting assets, optimizing assets, implementing backups and versioning, and defining asset collaboration workflows are key components of effective asset management. By adopting these practices, you can ensure that your project remains organized, efficient, and manageable throughout its development lifecycle.

1.5 Leveraging CryEngine Updates and New Releases

Keeping up to date with CryEngine's updates and new releases is vital for ensuring that your game development projects remain competitive and benefit from the latest features, improvements, and bug fixes. In this section, we'll explore strategies for effectively leveraging CryEngine updates.

Staying Informed

To take advantage of CryEngine updates, you must stay informed about the latest developments. Follow CryEngine's official communication channels, such as their website, forums, social media accounts, and mailing lists. Subscribe to newsletters and announcements to receive timely updates directly from the CryEngine team.

```
**Official CryEngine Communication Channels:**
- Website: [CryEngine Official Website](https://www.cryengine.com/)
```

- Forums: [CryEngine Community Forums](https://forum.cryengine.com/)
- Social Media: Follow CryEngine on Twitter, Facebook, and LinkedIn
- Mailing Lists: Subscribe to CryEngine newsletters for news and updates

Release Notes and Documentation

When a new CryEngine version is released, carefully review the release notes and documentation. This provides insights into new features, enhancements, and changes. Understanding the release notes helps you identify which updates are most relevant to your projects.

Example Release Note Highlights:
- CryEngine 5.7 Release:
  - Added Real-Time Global Illumination (RTGI) support
  - Improved asset import/export performance
  - Enhanced AI pathfinding algorithms

Compatibility Testing

Before upgrading to a new CryEngine version, perform compatibility testing with your existing project. Verify that your project's assets, scripts, and custom tools function correctly with the new version. Address any issues or incompatibilities to ensure a smooth transition.

Compatibility Testing Checklist:
- Test project functionality with CryEngine version
- Verify asset imports and rendering
- Test custom scripts and tools
- Ensure third-party plugins remain compatible

Version Control and Branching

Consider using version control branching strategies to manage CryEngine updates. Create a separate branch for testing and integrating the new version. This approach allows you to isolate update-related changes while keeping your main project stable.

```
# Git branching for CryEngine update
git checkout -b cryengine-update-5.7
```

Backward Compatibility

CryEngine often maintains backward compatibility with older project versions. However, it's essential to check for any deprecated features or deprecated API calls in your project code and assets. Update them to comply with the new version's requirements.

```
// Deprecated function in CryEngine 5.7
function deprecatedFunction() {
    // Deprecated functionality
}
```

Community Feedback

Engage with the CryEngine community to gather insights from other developers who have already updated their projects. Online forums, discussion boards, and social media groups provide valuable feedback and solutions to common issues encountered during updates.

```
**Community Feedback:**
- CryEngine Community Forum Thread: "CryEngine 5.7 Update Experiences"
- Reddit CryEngine Developers Group
- CryEngine Discord Server
```

Create a Update Plan

Develop a comprehensive update plan that outlines the steps and timeline for integrating the new CryEngine version into your project. Consider factors such as testing phases, bug fixing, and potential feature adoption. A well-structured plan minimizes disruptions to your project's development.

```
**Update Plan Phases:**
1. Research and Review
2. Compatibility Testing
3. Bug Fixing and Asset Updates
4. Integration and Deployment
```

Monitoring Hotfixes

CryEngine updates may come with hotfixes addressing critical issues. Keep an eye on hotfix releases and apply them as needed to ensure project stability and security. Hotfixes can resolve issues that might affect your project's development.

```
**Hotfix Application:**
- Monitor CryEngine website and forums for hotfix announcements
- Apply hotfixes promptly to address critical issues
```

In conclusion, leveraging CryEngine updates and new releases is essential for staying competitive in the game development industry. By staying informed, reviewing release notes, performing compatibility testing, managing version control, addressing backward compatibility, seeking community feedback, creating a comprehensive update plan, and monitoring hotfixes, you can ensure a smooth and successful transition to the latest CryEngine version, enhancing the quality and features of your projects.

Chapter 2: Advanced Level Design Concepts

2.1 Creating Complex and Dynamic Game Worlds

In this section, we will explore advanced level design concepts in CryEngine, focusing on the creation of complex and dynamic game worlds. Level design plays a crucial role in shaping the player's experience, and mastering these concepts will elevate your game design skills.

Level Design as Player Experience

Effective level design goes beyond aesthetics; it considers the player's experience. Advanced level designers craft environments that engage players emotionally and intellectually. They balance challenges, exploration, and storytelling to create memorable experiences.

```
// Level design for emotional engagement
- Emotional highs and lows
- Pacing of encounters
- Environmental storytelling
```

Modular Level Building

Modular level design involves creating reusable building blocks, such as rooms, corridors, and props, that can be assembled like LEGO pieces to construct game levels. This approach streamlines level creation and ensures consistency.

```
// Modular level design components
- Modular building sets
- Reusable assets
- Efficient asset management
```

Non-Linear Level Progression

Non-linear level design provides players with choices and multiple paths to explore. This design philosophy promotes player agency, allowing them to approach challenges and objectives in their preferred order.

```
// Non-linear level progression
- Branching paths
- Optional objectives
- Player decision-making
```

Dynamic Environments

Creating dynamic environments involves implementing interactive elements that respond to player actions or scripted events. Advanced level designers use CryEngine's tools to add elements like destructible objects, interactive switches, and environmental hazards.

```
// Dynamic environment elements
- Destructible objects
- Interactive switches
- Dynamic weather systems
```

Environmental Storytelling

Environmental storytelling is a narrative technique where the game world itself conveys a story. Expert level designers use props, environmental details, and level layout to tell a story without relying solely on dialogue or cutscenes.

```
// Environmental storytelling techniques
- Abandoned locations with clues
- Visual storytelling through props
- Hints and secrets hidden in the environment
```

Vertical Level Design

Vertical level design considers the use of height and vertical space within a level. This can involve multi-level structures, vertical puzzles, or varied elevation for combat encounters.

```
// Vertical level design principles
- Multi-level structures
- Climbing and traversal mechanics
- Vertical combat encounters
```

Level Optimization

Efficient level design includes optimization techniques to ensure smooth gameplay performance. This involves managing assets, culling unnecessary details, and using level streaming to load and unload parts of the level dynamically.

```
// Level optimization strategies
- Asset LODs
- Occlusion culling
- Streaming for large environments
```

Playtesting and Iteration

Advanced level designers recognize the importance of playtesting and iteration. They gather feedback from playtesters, identify pain points, and iterate on level designs to improve player experience continually.

```
**Playtesting and Iteration Process:**
1. Playtest with a focus group
2. Collect feedback and observations
3. Analyze player behavior and reactions
4. Iterate on level design based on feedback
```

Collaborative Level Design

Collaboration is key in complex level design. Level designers often work closely with artists, programmers, and writers to ensure that the level aligns with the overall game vision. Effective communication and teamwork are essential.

```
**Collaborative Level Design:**
- Regular team meetings
- Clear communication channels
- Asset and script integration
- Iterative design reviews
```

In conclusion, advanced level design in CryEngine involves creating complex and dynamic game worlds that engage players on multiple levels. It encompasses player experience, modular building, non-linear progression, dynamic environments, environmental storytelling, vertical design, optimization, playtesting, and collaboration. By mastering these concepts, you can craft immersive and memorable game levels that enhance the overall gaming experience.

2.2 Innovative Level Design Techniques

In this section, we will explore innovative level design techniques that go beyond traditional approaches. Advanced level designers often push the boundaries of creativity and interactivity to create unique and engaging game worlds.

Procedural Level Generation

Procedural level generation involves using algorithms and rules to generate game levels dynamically. This technique offers endless possibilities and replayability. Advanced level designers implement procedural generation to create diverse and unpredictable environments.

```
// Procedural level generation steps
1. Define procedural generation rules
2. Generate terrain, structures, and assets
3. Populate levels with enemies and items
4. Ensure balanced gameplay
```

Puzzle and Riddle Integration

Incorporating puzzles and riddles into level design challenges players' problem-solving skills and adds depth to the gameplay. Advanced level designers create puzzles that are seamlessly integrated into the game world, offering clues and challenges that blend with the narrative.

```
// Puzzle and riddle integration techniques
- Environmental clues
```

- Narrative-driven puzzles
- Physics-based puzzles

Interactive NPCs and Dialogues

Advanced level designers make NPCs and dialogues an integral part of level design. Interactive NPCs with rich dialogues and behaviors can enhance storytelling and create immersive experiences. The player's interactions with NPCs may influence the game's outcome.

```
// Interactive NPC design elements
- Scripted NPC behaviors
- Dialogue trees and choices
- Quests and side missions
```

Gravity and Physics Manipulation

Manipulating gravity and physics within a level can introduce unique gameplay mechanics. Gravity puzzles, zero-gravity environments, and physics-based challenges add variety and excitement to gameplay.

```
// Gravity and physics manipulation ideas
- Switchable gravity zones
- Zero-gravity traversal
- Physics-based traps and obstacles
```

Time Manipulation

Time manipulation mechanics can introduce innovative gameplay elements. Level designers experiment with time travel, time loops, or time-based puzzles that require players to alter the past or future to progress.

```
// Time manipulation gameplay features
- Time-traveling devices
- Time-locked areas
- Chronological puzzle-solving
```

Environmental Transformation

Transforming the game environment dynamically can keep players engaged and surprised. This technique involves altering the level's appearance, layout, or challenges in real-time.

```
// Environmental transformation mechanics
- Day-night cycles
- Dynamic weather systems
- Transformable structures and terrain
```

Esoteric Navigation and Traversal

Advanced level designers design levels that challenge players' navigation skills with unconventional traversal methods. This can include parkour, climbing, and wall-running mechanics.

```
// Esoteric navigation and traversal elements
- Parkour-friendly level architecture
- Climbing challenges
- Wall-running sections
```

Time-Driven Events and Consequences

Introducing time-driven events and consequences adds depth to level design. Decisions made by players may trigger specific events or change the course of the game's narrative.

```
// Time-driven events and consequences
- Timed escape sequences
- Time-sensitive decision-making
- Dynamic branching storylines
```

Parallel Dimensions and Realities

Parallel dimensions and alternate realities can create mind-bending level design experiences. Level designers craft levels where players can shift between different dimensions, each with its own rules and challenges.

```
// Parallel dimensions and reality shifts
- Parallel worlds with distinct properties
- Puzzle-solving through dimension hopping
- Altered physics and environment in different dimensions
```

In conclusion, innovative level design techniques push the boundaries of traditional game design, offering players fresh and engaging experiences. Procedural level generation, puzzles and riddles, interactive NPCs, gravity and physics manipulation, time manipulation, environmental transformation, esoteric navigation, time-driven events, and parallel dimensions are just a few of the techniques advanced level designers employ to create unique and memorable game worlds. By incorporating these techniques, you can captivate players and offer them exciting and thought-provoking gameplay experiences.

2.3 Environmental Storytelling in Depth

Environmental storytelling is a powerful narrative technique that allows level designers to convey a story, history, or context without relying on explicit dialogue or cutscenes. In this section, we'll delve deep into the art of environmental storytelling in CryEngine and explore how it can enrich your game worlds.

The Essence of Environmental Storytelling

At its core, environmental storytelling involves using the game environment itself to communicate information, evoke emotions, and immerse players in the game's world. It relies on subtle cues, visual details, and level design choices to tell a story indirectly.

```
// Key elements of environmental storytelling
- Visual cues and details
- Level layout and architecture
- Object placement and arrangement
```

World Building and Lore

Advanced level designers often begin by crafting a rich world with its own lore, history, and rules. This background information informs the design of the game world and allows for consistent and believable storytelling.

```
// Example world-building elements
- Fictional history and events
- Cultural backgrounds
- Unique flora and fauna
```

Visual Storytelling Elements

Visual storytelling involves using the environment's visual elements to convey information. This can include:

- **Environmental Props**: Objects and items placed in the level that tell a story through their placement and condition. For example, a broken carriage on a deserted road suggests an ambush.

- **Set Dressing**: Arranging the environment with specific items, such as books, documents, or graffiti, to hint at the game's lore or provide clues to players.

- **Environmental Changes**: Progressive changes in the environment that reflect the narrative, such as a town gradually falling into disrepair as a story unfolds.

```
// Visual storytelling through set dressing
- Abandoned campsite with diary entries
- Ruined buildings with faded propaganda posters
- Overgrown garden with a hidden tombstone
```

Spatial Arrangement and Flow

The layout of a level can itself tell a story. Advanced level designers consider the spatial arrangement of areas, the flow of progression, and the juxtaposition of different spaces to create a narrative journey.

```
// Spatial storytelling techniques
- Using level architecture to guide players
- Creating memorable landmarks and vistas
- Changing atmosphere as players progress
```

Narrative Puzzles and Secrets

Environmental storytelling can also involve hidden puzzles, secrets, or easter eggs that players can discover. These elements add depth to the narrative and encourage exploration.

```
// Narrative puzzles and secrets
- Hidden journals revealing backstory
- Environmental puzzles tied to the lore
- Secret rooms with unique items or clues
```

Dynamic Environmental Changes

Advanced level designers may implement dynamic changes in the environment as the story unfolds. This could include environmental destruction, weather changes, or the gradual transformation of a location to reflect the narrative's progression.

```
// Dynamic environmental storytelling
- Destructible buildings during a battle
- Changing weather patterns for dramatic effect
- Areas that evolve over time in response to player choices
```

Player Engagement and Interpretation

One of the strengths of environmental storytelling is that it engages players' imagination and encourages them to interpret the narrative themselves. This can lead to player discussions, theories, and a deeper connection to the game world.

```
**Player Engagement and Interpretation:**
- Players discussing environmental clues
- Fan theories and speculation
- Player-created lore and backstory
```

Storytelling Consistency

Maintaining consistency in environmental storytelling is crucial. Advanced level designers ensure that the environmental details align with the overarching narrative and that players can make meaningful connections between elements.

```
// Consistency in environmental storytelling
- Continuity in environmental changes
- Clarity in visual cues and hints
- Avoiding narrative contradictions within the environment
```

In conclusion, environmental storytelling is a nuanced and powerful technique in CryEngine level design. It allows level designers to create immersive and evocative game worlds that captivate players' imaginations and deepen their connection to the narrative. By mastering the art of environmental storytelling and carefully crafting each element of the game environment, you can provide players with a rich and engaging storytelling experience.

2.4 Balancing Aesthetics and Functionality

In advanced level design, achieving the right balance between aesthetics and functionality is paramount. A game level should not only look visually appealing but also serve the gameplay, narrative, and player experience. In this section, we'll explore the strategies and considerations for achieving this balance in CryEngine.

The Interplay of Aesthetics and Functionality

Aesthetics and functionality are not mutually exclusive in level design. They can complement each other when approached strategically. A visually stunning environment can enhance player immersion, while functional design elements ensure a smooth and engaging gameplay experience.

```
// Key considerations for balancing aesthetics and functionality
- Player navigation and readability
- Narrative cohesion and visual storytelling
- Gameplay mechanics and challenges
```

Player Navigation and Readability

A well-designed level should guide players intuitively. Visual cues, lighting, and level architecture should help players understand where to go, what to interact with, and how to progress. Clarity in level design is crucial for player engagement.

```
// Strategies for player navigation and readability
- Clearly defined paths and routes
- Visual markers and waypoints
- Highlighted interactive elements
```

Narrative Cohesion and Visual Storytelling

Aesthetics can play a significant role in reinforcing the game's narrative. The visual elements of a level, such as architecture, props, and environmental details, should align with the game's story, setting, and characters.

```
// Techniques for narrative cohesion and visual storytelling
- Consistent architectural styles
- Thematically relevant props and decorations
- Environmental details that reflect the narrative background
```

Gameplay Mechanics and Challenges

Functionality is closely tied to gameplay mechanics and challenges. Advanced level designers ensure that the level layout, obstacles, and interactive elements serve the intended gameplay experience. Balancing difficulty and player progression is vital.

```
// Integrating gameplay mechanics and challenges
- Purposeful placement of obstacles and enemies
- Puzzles and interactions aligned with the story
- Level pacing that matches the gameplay rhythm
```

Consistency in Art Style

Aesthetically pleasing levels often follow a consistent art style or theme. Maintaining this consistency throughout the level ensures that players remain immersed and that the visual elements align with the game's identity.

```
// Consistency in art style considerations
- Adherence to the game's art direction
- Maintaining a cohesive color palette
- Consistent lighting and shading techniques
```

Lighting and Atmosphere

Lighting plays a critical role in both aesthetics and functionality. Properly lit levels not only look visually appealing but also influence the mood and atmosphere of the gameplay. Lighting can be used strategically to guide player attention and create focal points.

```
// Utilizing lighting for aesthetics and functionality
- Dynamic lighting effects for dramatic scenes
- Subtle lighting cues to highlight interactive elements
- Atmospheric lighting to evoke specific emotions
```

Optimization for Performance

Balancing aesthetics and functionality also involves optimizing the level for performance. Complex visuals and detailed environments should not negatively impact the game's frame rate or player experience. Level designers often implement techniques like LODs (Level of Detail) and efficient asset management to maintain performance.

```
// Performance optimization strategies
- Asset LODs to reduce rendering load
- Texture and mesh optimization
- Occlusion culling to limit rendering of unseen areas
```

Iteration and Playtesting

Achieving the right balance between aesthetics and functionality often requires iterative design and playtesting. Level designers gather feedback from playtesters to identify areas where improvements are needed, whether in terms of aesthetics, functionality, or both.

```
**Iteration and Playtesting Process:**
1. Design and implement level elements
2. Conduct playtests with a focus group
3. Collect feedback on aesthetics and functionality
4. Iterate on level design based on feedback
```

Collaboration between level designers, artists, and programmers is essential for achieving the balance between aesthetics and functionality. Effective communication and teamwork ensure that the visual and functional aspects of the level align with the overall game vision.

```
**Collaborative Approach:**
- Regular team meetings to discuss design and functionality
- Artist input on aesthetics and visual elements
- Programmer support for interactive features and mechanics
- Iterative design reviews with the team
```

In conclusion, balancing aesthetics and functionality is a core challenge in advanced level design within CryEngine. Striking the right balance ensures that your game levels not only look visually stunning but also enhance player engagement, narrative cohesion, and gameplay experiences. By considering player navigation, narrative cohesion, gameplay mechanics, art style consistency, lighting, performance optimization, iteration, and collaboration, you can create game levels that are both aesthetically pleasing and highly functional.

2.5 Integrating Levels with Narrative and Gameplay

Effective integration of game levels with the overarching narrative and gameplay mechanics is a critical aspect of advanced level design in CryEngine. In this section, we'll explore strategies and techniques for ensuring that your levels seamlessly connect with the game's story and provide engaging gameplay experiences.

Aligning Levels with Narrative

A cohesive narrative is essential for player immersion. Advanced level designers work closely with writers and narrative designers to ensure that each level contributes to the game's story progression. The level's setting, events, and characters should align with the narrative.

```
// Strategies for aligning levels with the narrative
- Consistent character motivations and actions
- Environments that reflect the story's world
- Maintaining a logical timeline of events
```

Narrative Pacing and Player Progression

Levels should be paced to match the narrative's rhythm and the player's progression. Some levels may focus on character development, while others provide intense action sequences. Advanced level designers carefully plan the pacing to keep players engaged.

```
// Techniques for narrative pacing and player progression
- Mixing exploration, combat, and story-driven segments
- Using cutscenes and scripted events to control pacing
- Allowing players to make choices that impact the story
```

Character Interaction and Development

Integrating characters into level design enriches the narrative. Conversations, interactions, and character development moments can occur within the level itself. Players should feel that the characters' actions and dialogues are influenced by the environment.

```
// Methods for character interaction and development in levels
- Dynamic character dialogues based on player choices
- Character behaviors influenced by the environment
- Staging character encounters in thematic locations
```

Gameplay Mechanics Alignment

Levels must align with the game's core gameplay mechanics. This includes ensuring that the level's design supports the use of player abilities, weapons, and tools. Gameplay challenges and puzzles should be seamlessly integrated into the level's environment.

```
// Aligning level design with gameplay mechanics
- Designing levels that encourage skill-based gameplay
- Introducing level-specific mechanics and challenges
- Integrating puzzles that require player abilities
```

Environmental Storytelling

Environmental storytelling is an effective way to immerse players in the narrative. Level designers use visual cues, props, and environmental details to convey backstory and plot elements indirectly. Players should feel that the environment itself tells a story.

```
// Utilizing environmental storytelling techniques
- Placing objects and documents that hint at the narrative
- Creating visually memorable locations tied to the story
- Using environmental changes to reflect the narrative's progression
```

Consistency in Worldbuilding

Levels should fit seamlessly within the game's world and lore. Advanced level designers adhere to the established rules, cultures, and histories of the game's universe. Consistency in worldbuilding ensures that players remain immersed in a coherent and believable game world.

```
// Maintaining worldbuilding consistency
- Adhering to established lore and rules
- Ensuring architectural styles match the game's world
- Using thematically relevant props and decorations
```

Branching Narratives and Player Choices

Some games feature branching narratives and player choices that impact the story's outcome. Level designers must create levels that accommodate these choices and provide different experiences based on player decisions.

```
// Designing levels for branching narratives and player choices
- Multiple paths and objectives within a level
- Unique dialogues and interactions based on choices
- Ensuring the consequences of choices affect future levels
```

Playtesting and Iteration

Playtesting is essential to identify and address issues in the integration of levels with narrative and gameplay. Advanced level designers conduct playtests to gather feedback, ensure narrative coherence, and refine gameplay experiences through iteration.

```
**Playtesting and Iteration Process:**
1. Playtest the level with a focus group
2. Collect feedback on narrative integration and gameplay
3. Analyze player behavior and narrative comprehension
4. Iterate on level design to improve alignment
```

Collaborative Development

Effective collaboration between level designers, writers, narrative designers, and gameplay designers is crucial. Regular communication and coordination ensure that levels seamlessly blend with the game's overall vision.

```
**Collaborative Development Approach:**
- Ongoing discussions between level designers and narrative writers
- Collaboration on character dialogues and behaviors
- Consistent alignment with the game's core vision
- Iterative design reviews with the development team
```

In conclusion, advanced level design in CryEngine demands a deep integration of levels with narrative and gameplay elements. It requires careful alignment with the game's story, pacing, character interactions, and gameplay mechanics. By implementing these strategies and techniques, you can create game levels that enhance the player's immersion and contribute meaningfully to the overall gaming experience.

Chapter 3: High-End Programming in CryEngine

3.1 Advanced Scripting with Lua and C++

In this section, we will explore the world of advanced scripting in CryEngine using both Lua and C++. Scripting is a crucial aspect of game development, allowing you to implement custom gameplay mechanics, create interactive systems, and bring your game to life with dynamic behaviors.

Scripting Languages in CryEngine

CryEngine supports two primary scripting languages: Lua and C++. Each has its strengths and use cases within game development.

Lua: Lua is a lightweight, embeddable scripting language known for its simplicity and flexibility. It's commonly used for scripting gameplay logic, AI behavior, and user interface elements. Lua scripts are often more accessible to non-programmers, making it a preferred choice for rapid iteration and prototyping.

```lua
-- Example Lua script for a simple player character behavior
function OnUpdate(deltaTime)
    local player = GetPlayerEntity()
    if player then
        local position = player:GetWorldPos()
        position.x = position.x + 1.0 * deltaTime
        player:SetWorldPos(position)
    end
end
```

C++: CryEngine also allows for low-level programming using C++. While C++ development can be more complex, it provides high performance and direct access to engine internals. C++ is typically used for creating custom engine features, optimizations, and complex game systems.

```cpp
// Example C++ code for a custom CryEngine component
#include "GamePlugin.h"

class CustomComponent : public IEntityComponent
{
public:
    CustomComponent() {}
    ~CustomComponent() {}

    void Initialize() override {}
    void ProcessEvent(SEntityEvent& event) override {}
};
```

Advanced scripting goes beyond basic functionality and explores more complex techniques to achieve specific gameplay goals.

State Machines: Implementing state machines in scripts allows you to manage complex AI behaviors, character states, and interactive systems. State machines define different states and transitions between them, providing a structured approach to handling game logic.

```lua
-- Example Lua code for an AI state machine
local currentState = "Patrol"

function OnUpdate(deltaTime)
    if currentState == "Patrol" then
        -- AI patrols a predefined path
        -- Check conditions for transitioning to other states
        if ShouldAttackPlayer() then
            currentState = "Attack"
        elseif ShouldIdle() then
            currentState = "Idle"
        end
    elseif currentState == "Attack" then
        -- AI attacks the player
        -- Handle transitions to other states
    elseif currentState == "Idle" then
        -- AI idles and waits
        -- Handle transitions to other states
    end
end
```

Event Handling: Advanced scripting involves setting up event-driven systems where specific events trigger scripted responses. Events can include player interactions, object interactions, or in-game triggers.

```lua
-- Example Lua code for event handling in a puzzle game
function OnPlayerInteract(object)
    if IsPuzzlePiece(object) then
        -- Handle interaction with puzzle piece
        -- Check if the puzzle is complete
        if IsPuzzleComplete() then
            TriggerEvent("PuzzleComplete")
        end
    end
end

function OnEvent(eventType)
    if eventType == "PuzzleComplete" then
        -- Execute actions when the puzzle is complete
    end
end
```

Optimization and Performance: Advanced scripting also includes techniques for optimizing script performance. This may involve optimizing loops, reducing unnecessary computations, and managing memory efficiently, especially when working with C++ code.

```cpp
// Example C++ code for optimizing script performance
void UpdateAIEntities()
{
    for (EntityId entityId : m_AIEntities)
    {
        if (IsEntityActive(entityId))
        {
            UpdateAIBehavior(entityId);
        }
        else
        {
            // Remove inactive entities from the list to optimize processing
            RemoveEntity(entityId);
        }
    }
}
```

Debugging and Testing

Advanced scripting often involves more intricate logic, which can lead to complex bugs. CryEngine provides debugging tools to aid in identifying and fixing issues in your scripts. Using breakpoints, logging, and testing in a controlled environment can help ensure the reliability of your scripts.

```lua
-- Example Lua code with debugging using print statements
function OnUpdate(deltaTime)
    -- Debug information to track script behavior
    Print("Updating AI logic")
    local player = GetPlayerEntity()
    if player then
        Print("Player entity found")
        -- Additional debug information
    end
end
```

In conclusion, advanced scripting with Lua and C++ in CryEngine empowers game developers to create dynamic and complex gameplay systems, AI behaviors, and interactive experiences. Whether you choose Lua for rapid prototyping or C++ for performance-critical components, mastering scripting techniques is essential for achieving your game's vision and providing players with engaging and interactive content.

3.2 Custom Gameplay Mechanics and Systems

In this section, we will delve into the creation of custom gameplay mechanics and systems using CryEngine. Advanced game development often requires unique gameplay elements that set your game apart and provide players with engaging experiences. Custom gameplay mechanics can range from complex character abilities to innovative puzzle systems, and this section will guide you through the process.

Identifying Gameplay Needs

Before diving into implementing custom gameplay mechanics, it's crucial to identify the specific needs of your game. Consider the following questions:

- What core gameplay mechanics define your game's identity?
- Are there unique abilities or interactions that differentiate your characters or objects?
- How can custom gameplay mechanics enhance the player experience and overall gameplay flow?

Designing Custom Mechanics

Once you've identified the gameplay needs, the next step is to design the mechanics themselves. Start by defining the rules, behaviors, and interactions of your custom mechanics. Consider how they fit into the larger gameplay ecosystem and how they align with the game's narrative and objectives.

Design Considerations:
- Defining rules and constraints
- Balancing mechanics for player challenge
- Ensuring mechanics support the game's goals

Scripting Custom Mechanics

Implementing custom gameplay mechanics often involves scripting. CryEngine supports both Lua and C++ for scripting, allowing you to choose the best fit for your specific mechanics. Writing scripts that control the behavior of characters, objects, or systems is a fundamental part of creating custom gameplay.

```lua
-- Example Lua script for a custom character ability
function OnUseSpecialAbility(player)
    if player and CanUseSpecialAbility(player) then
        -- Execute the custom ability logic here
        PerformSpecialAbility(player)
    end
end
```

```cpp
// Example C++ code for a custom gameplay system
#include "GamePlugin.h"

class CustomGameplaySystem
```

```
{
public:
    CustomGameplaySystem() {}
    ~CustomGameplaySystem() {}

    void Initialize() {}
    void Update(float deltaTime) {}
    void HandleInput(const SInputEvent& inputEvent) {}
};
```

Player Feedback and User Interface

Custom gameplay mechanics should provide clear feedback to players. This includes visual cues, audio effects, and user interface elements that inform players about the mechanics' status and outcomes. Effective feedback enhances player understanding and engagement.

```
**Player Feedback Elements:**
- Visual effects and animations
- Sound effects and audio cues
- HUD elements and UI prompts
```

Testing and Iteration

Thorough testing and iteration are essential when implementing custom gameplay mechanics. Playtest your mechanics extensively to identify any issues or areas for improvement. Player feedback during testing can also lead to refinements that enhance the mechanics' fun factor and balance.

```
**Testing and Iteration Process:**
1. Implement the mechanics in a test environment.
2. Invite playtesters to experience and provide feedback.
3. Analyze player behavior and identify any pain points.
4. Iteratively refine the mechanics based on feedback.
```

Documentation and Communication

As you develop custom gameplay mechanics, it's vital to document their functionality and requirements. Clear documentation helps team members understand how to use and work with the mechanics. Effective communication within the development team ensures everyone is on the same page regarding the mechanics' design and implementation.

```
**Documentation and Communication:**
- Creating design documents for mechanics
- Writing code comments and documentation
- Holding regular team meetings to discuss progress
```

Performance Optimization

Custom gameplay mechanics should be optimized for performance, especially if they involve complex calculations or interactions. Ensure that your scripts or code are efficient and do not introduce performance bottlenecks.

```cpp
// Example C++ code for optimizing custom gameplay mechanics
void UpdateCustomMechanics(float deltaTime)
{
    // Perform efficient calculations and updates
    // Avoid unnecessary iterations or heavy computations
    // Implement optimizations like object pooling when applicable
}
```

Post-Launch Support and Updates

Once your game is released, continue to support and update your custom gameplay mechanics as needed. Player feedback and evolving gameplay dynamics may require adjustments to maintain a balanced and engaging experience.

```
**Post-Launch Support:**
- Monitoring player feedback and analytics
- Identifying issues and addressing them through patches or updates
- Adding new mechanics or enhancing existing ones to keep the game fresh
```

In conclusion, creating custom gameplay mechanics and systems is a fundamental aspect of advanced game development in CryEngine. By carefully designing, scripting, testing, and optimizing your mechanics, you can provide players with unique and engaging gameplay experiences that contribute to the success and appeal of your game.

3.3 Optimization and Memory Management

Optimization and memory management are critical aspects of high-end programming in CryEngine. Ensuring that your game runs smoothly and efficiently is essential for delivering a polished and enjoyable player experience. In this section, we'll explore strategies and best practices for optimizing your CryEngine project and managing memory effectively.

Profiling and Performance Analysis

Before diving into optimization, it's crucial to profile your game to identify performance bottlenecks. CryEngine provides profiling tools and performance analysis features that help you pinpoint areas of your game that need improvement.

```
**Profiling and Analysis Tools:**
- CryEngine Profiler for CPU and GPU performance analysis
- Memory analysis tools for tracking memory usage
- Real-time frame rate monitoring and profiling
```

Scripting Optimization

Optimizing your scripts is a key step in improving gameplay performance. Inefficient scripts can lead to frame rate drops and gameplay hiccups. Here are some scripting optimization techniques:

- **Reduce Script Complexity:** Simplify complex scripts by breaking them into smaller functions or optimizing loops and calculations.

- **Object Pooling:** Use object pooling to recycle and reuse objects rather than constantly creating and destroying them. This reduces memory allocation overhead.

- **Asynchronous Operations:** Offload time-consuming operations to separate threads or coroutines to keep the main game loop smooth.

```lua
-- Example Lua code for object pooling
local objectPool = {}

function CreateObject()
    local object = table.remove(objectPool) or CreateNewObject()
    object:Reset()
    return object
end

function RecycleObject(object)
    table.insert(objectPool, object)
end
```

Texture and Asset Optimization

Texture and asset management play a significant role in optimizing memory usage and loading times. CryEngine provides tools for optimizing textures and assets for better performance:

- **Texture Compression:** Use texture compression formats to reduce the size of textures without significant loss of quality.

- **Texture Streaming:** Implement texture streaming to load textures as needed, reducing memory usage.

- **LODs (Level of Detail):** Create multiple levels of detail for assets to reduce rendering load when objects are at a distance.

```
**Texture and Asset Optimization Tips:**
- Use appropriate texture formats (DXT, BC, ETC) based on platform.
- Implement mipmap generation for textures.
- Use LODs for static and dynamic objects.
```

Effective memory management is vital to prevent memory leaks and optimize resource usage. CryEngine provides tools to help manage memory effectively:

- **Reference Counting:** Properly manage reference counting to release resources when they are no longer in use.

- **Memory Allocation Tracking:** Use memory allocation tracking tools to identify and address memory leaks.

- **Resource Unloading:** Implement mechanisms to unload unused or unnecessary assets and data from memory.

```cpp
// Example C++ code for memory management using reference counting
class RefCountedObject
{
public:
    RefCountedObject() : m_refCount(1) {}
    virtual ~RefCountedObject() {}

    void AddRef() { ++m_refCount; }
    void Release()
    {
        if (--m_refCount <= 0)
            delete this;
    }

private:
    int m_refCount;
};
```

CPU and GPU Optimization

Optimizing CPU and GPU usage is essential for maintaining a consistent frame rate and responsiveness. CryEngine provides tools to analyze and optimize CPU and GPU performance:

- **Multithreading:** Utilize multithreading to distribute CPU workload and improve performance.

- **Shader Optimization:** Optimize shaders to reduce GPU load by minimizing redundant calculations and shader complexity.

- **Batching:** Group rendering calls into batches to reduce CPU overhead.

```
**CPU and GPU Optimization Strategies:**
- Profile CPU and GPU usage to identify bottlenecks.
- Use efficient data structures and algorithms in your code.
- Limit the number of draw calls and minimize state changes for rendering.
```

Streaming and Loading Optimization

Optimizing asset streaming and loading is crucial for maintaining seamless gameplay. CryEngine provides tools to streamline asset loading and optimize streaming:

- **Streaming Levels:** Organize your levels into streaming chunks to load only what is necessary for the player's current location.

- **Background Loading:** Implement background loading to load assets asynchronously while the game is running.

- **Resource Prefetching:** Predictively load resources that are likely to be needed soon, reducing load times during gameplay.

```
**Streaming and Loading Optimization Tips:**
- Balance the quality of loaded assets with loading times.
- Implement level of detail (LOD) for streaming assets.
- Use background loading for non-essential assets.
```

Platform-Specific Optimization

Optimization requirements can vary across different gaming platforms and hardware configurations. Ensure that your optimizations are tailored to the platform(s) you are targeting. Test and profile your game on each platform to address platform-specific performance issues.

```
**Platform-Specific Optimization Considerations:**
- Adjust graphics settings and asset quality for different platforms.
- Optimize for different CPU architectures and memory constraints.
- Utilize platform-specific rendering features and APIs.
```

Continuous Optimization

Optimization is an ongoing process throughout the development cycle. Regularly profile, test, and optimize your game to ensure that it meets performance targets. Addressing performance issues early in development can save time and resources in the long run.

```
**Continuous Optimization Approach:**
- Schedule regular profiling and performance analysis sessions.
- Act on feedback from playtesters regarding performance.
- Stay up to date with CryEngine updates and optimization features.
```

In conclusion, optimization and memory management are integral parts of advanced programming in CryEngine. By profiling your game, optimizing scripts, managing assets efficiently, and addressing CPU and GPU bottlenecks, you can create a smooth and responsive gaming experience for players while ensuring that your game runs optimally across various platforms.

3.4 Multi-threading and Performance Enhancements

Multi-threading is a powerful technique in CryEngine that can significantly improve performance by distributing tasks across multiple CPU cores. In this section, we will explore the benefits of multi-threading and various strategies for enhancing performance in your CryEngine project.

The Importance of Multi-threading

Modern game engines like CryEngine rely on multi-threading to maximize CPU utilization and ensure smooth gameplay. By breaking down tasks into smaller threads, you can take advantage of multi-core processors and distribute computational workloads efficiently.

Parallelization of Game Logic

Multi-threading in CryEngine can be applied to parallelize various aspects of game logic, including physics simulation, AI calculations, and rendering tasks. Here are some examples:

- **Physics Simulation:** Multi-threading allows for concurrent physics calculations, improving the accuracy and responsiveness of physical interactions in the game.

- **AI Processing:** Distributing AI computations across threads enables more complex and responsive enemy behaviors, enhancing the overall gameplay experience.

- **Rendering:** Parallelizing rendering tasks can boost frame rates and reduce frame time, resulting in smoother graphics performance.

Threading Models in CryEngine

CryEngine supports different threading models to cater to various aspects of game development:

- **Job System:** The job system in CryEngine is designed to efficiently manage parallel tasks. You can create jobs to be executed in parallel, making it easier to leverage multi-core processors.

```cpp
// Example C++ code for creating and running a job in CryEngine
CJobSystem::AddJob([]()
{
    // Perform parallelized task here
});
```

- **Task Graph System:** CryEngine's task graph system offers a more high-level approach to task parallelism. It allows you to define dependencies between tasks, ensuring proper synchronization.

```cpp
// Example C++ code for creating tasks in the task graph system
void MyTaskGraphFunction(ITaskGraph* pTaskGraph)
{
    // Define tasks and their dependencies
    TaskID task1 = pTaskGraph->AddTask(TaskFunction1);
    TaskID task2 = pTaskGraph->AddTask(TaskFunction2);
```

```
    // Specify dependencies between tasks
    pTaskGraph->SetDependency(task2, task1);

    // Execute the task graph
    pTaskGraph->Execute();
}
```

Load Balancing

Efficient multi-threading requires load balancing to ensure that each core is utilized optimally. Load balancing involves distributing tasks evenly among available threads, preventing any single thread from becoming a bottleneck.

- **Dynamic Load Balancing:** CryEngine employs dynamic load balancing techniques to adjust the distribution of tasks based on the current workload and available CPU cores.

- **Task Prioritization:** Some tasks may have higher priority, such as physics calculations during gameplay. Prioritizing tasks ensures that critical computations are processed promptly.

```
// Example C++ code for dynamic Load balancing in CryEngine
CryMT::GetTaskManager()->SetDynamicTaskLoadBalancing(true);
```

Synchronization and Thread Safety

Multi-threading introduces the challenge of synchronization to ensure that threads do not access shared resources concurrently, which can lead to data corruption or crashes. CryEngine provides synchronization primitives like mutexes and semaphores to manage thread safety.

```
// Example C++ code for using a mutex in CryEngine for thread safety
CRY_CRITICAL_SECTION(MyCriticalSection);
CRYENTERSECTION(MyCriticalSection);
// Perform thread-safe operations
CRYEXITSECTION(MyCriticalSection);
```

Profiling and Optimization

To effectively harness the benefits of multi-threading, it's essential to profile and optimize your code regularly. Profiling tools in CryEngine can help identify performance bottlenecks and areas where multi-threading can be most beneficial.

- **Profiling Tools:** Use CryEngine's profiling tools to analyze CPU and GPU usage, thread performance, and identify areas for optimization.

- **Thread Affinity:** Assigning specific threads to certain tasks can help optimize performance further by ensuring that threads run on specific CPU cores.

```
// Example C++ code for setting thread affinity in CryEngine
CryThreadSetName("MyThread");
CryThreadSetAffinityMask(0x01); // Set thread affinity to CPU core 0
```

Platform Considerations

When implementing multi-threading in CryEngine, consider the target platforms and their hardware capabilities. Different platforms may have varying numbers of CPU cores, so it's essential to adapt your multi-threading strategy accordingly.

Continuous Testing and Iteration

Multi-threading and performance enhancements require ongoing testing and iteration. Regularly evaluate the impact of multi-threaded changes on gameplay and frame rates. Iterate on your multi-threading approach based on performance data and player feedback.

In conclusion, multi-threading is a powerful technique for enhancing performance in CryEngine. By parallelizing game logic, optimizing load balancing, ensuring thread safety, and utilizing profiling tools, you can take full advantage of multi-core processors and deliver a smoother and more responsive gaming experience to your players.

3.5 AI Programming: Creating Intelligent and Adaptive NPCs

Artificial Intelligence (AI) is a fundamental component of modern video games, contributing to the behavior and interaction of non-player characters (NPCs). In this section, we will explore AI programming in CryEngine, focusing on techniques to create intelligent and adaptive NPCs that enhance the player's gaming experience.

The Role of AI in Gaming

AI in games serves various purposes, including:

- **Enemy Behavior:** Creating challenging and dynamic enemy behavior, such as combat tactics, flanking, and evasion.

- **Ally Behavior:** Controlling the actions and decision-making of allied NPCs, ensuring they support the player effectively.

- **Environmental Interaction:** Enabling NPCs to interact with the game world, including pathfinding, navigation, and object manipulation.

Finite State Machines (FSMs)

Finite State Machines are a common method for modeling NPC behavior in games. FSMs define a set of states that NPCs can be in, along with transitions between these states based on specific conditions. This approach provides a structured way to implement intelligent and adaptive NPCs.

```lua
-- Example Lua code for an NPC FSM
local currentState = "Idle"

function OnUpdate(deltaTime)
    if currentState == "Idle" then
        -- Implement idle behavior
        if ShouldChasePlayer() then
            currentState = "Chase"
        elseif ShouldPatrol() then
            currentState = "Patrol"
        end
    elseif currentState == "Chase" then
        -- Implement chase behavior
        if ShouldReturnToIdle() then
            currentState = "Idle"
        end
    elseif currentState == "Patrol" then
        -- Implement patrol behavior
        if ShouldChasePlayer() then
            currentState = "Chase"
        end
    end
end
```

Behavior Trees

Behavior Trees are another popular approach to NPC AI programming. They consist of nodes representing actions, conditions, and composite nodes that define the flow of AI behavior. Behavior Trees offer flexibility and can handle complex decision-making.

```cpp
// Example C++ code for an AI Behavior Tree node
class ChasePlayerNode : public BehaviorNode
{
public:
    ChasePlayerNode() {}
    ~ChasePlayerNode() {}

    virtual BehaviorStatus Execute() override
    {
        // Implement logic to chase the player
        return BehaviorStatus::Success;
    }
};
```

Dynamic Decision-Making

Creating intelligent NPCs often involves dynamic decision-making based on changing circumstances. NPCs should adapt to different situations, such as combat, stealth, or interaction with the environment. This requires implementing decision-making algorithms that evaluate the current state and select appropriate actions.

```cpp
// Example C++ code for dynamic decision-making in AI
void UpdateAI()
{
    if (IsInCombat())
    {
        // Make combat-related decisions
        if (IsLowOnHealth())
            Flee();
        else
            Attack();
    }
    else if (IsInStealthMode())
    {
        // Perform stealth actions
        if (IsDetected())
            Escape();
        else
            Hide();
    }
    else
    {
        // Default behavior
        Wander();
    }
}
```

Learning and Adaptation

Advanced AI can incorporate learning and adaptation mechanisms. Machine learning algorithms, such as reinforcement learning or neural networks, can be applied to NPCs to improve their behavior over time. NPCs can learn from player interactions and adapt to different playstyles.

```
**Machine Learning in NPC AI:**
- Reinforcement learning for reward-based behavior.
- Neural networks for pattern recognition and decision-making.
- Genetic algorithms for evolving AI behaviors.
```

Pathfinding and Navigation

Efficient pathfinding and navigation are essential for NPCs to move intelligently within the game world. CryEngine provides built-in navigation systems and pathfinding algorithms that simplify the implementation of NPC movement.

```cpp
// Example C++ code for NPC pathfinding in CryEngine
void MoveToTarget(EntityId npcEntity, Vec3 targetPosition)
{
    IEntity* pEntity = gEnv->pEntitySystem->GetEntity(npcEntity);
    if (pEntity)
    {
        // Use CryEngine's navigation system to calculate the path
```

```
        INavigationSystem* pNavSystem = gEnv->pAISystem->GetNavigationSystem(
);

        INavPath* pPath = pNavSystem->CreateNavPath();
        pNavSystem->ComputePath(pPath, pEntity, targetPosition);

        // Follow the path by adjusting the NPC's position
        // ...
    }
}
```

Sensory Perception

NPCs in CryEngine can be equipped with sensory perception, including vision, hearing, and other senses. Implementing sensory systems allows NPCs to detect the player and other in-game elements, adding depth to their behavior.

```
// Example C++ code for NPC sensory perception in CryEngine
void UpdatePerception(EntityId npcEntity)
{
    IEntity* pEntity = gEnv->pEntitySystem->GetEntity(npcEntity);
    if (pEntity)
    {
        // Check for player presence using vision and hearing sensors
        // Update NPC behavior based on sensory input
        // ...
    }
}
```

Debugging and Testing

Testing and debugging AI behavior is crucial to ensure that NPCs behave as intended. Use debugging tools, such as visualization of AI states and decision-making processes, to identify and fix issues in NPC behavior.

```
**Debugging AI Behavior:**
- Visualizing AI states and transitions.
- Simulating player interactions for testing.
- Logging AI decision-making for analysis.
```

Player Experience Enhancement

Intelligent and adaptive NPCs contribute significantly to the player's overall experience

---

Chapter 4: Sophisticated Character Design and Animation

4.1 Advanced Character Modeling Techniques

Character modeling is a critical aspect of game development, contributing to the visual appeal and realism of characters in your CryEngine project. In this section, we will delve into advanced character modeling techniques, including high-quality character design and optimization.

Polygon Modeling

Polygon modeling remains a fundamental technique for character modeling in CryEngine. It involves creating characters by manipulating vertices, edges, and faces to form 3D models. To achieve high-quality character models, consider the following techniques:

- **Topological Flow:** Ensure that the edge loops and vertex placement follow the natural contours of the character, enhancing deformation during animation.

- **Retopologizing:** Optimize the character mesh by reducing unnecessary polygons while maintaining detail where needed.

- **UV Unwrapping:** Properly unwrap UV maps to facilitate texture painting and material assignment.

High-Resolution Sculpting

High-resolution sculpting allows artists to create intricate character details using sculpting software like ZBrush or Mudbox. These high-resolution sculpted details, such as wrinkles, pores, and muscle definition, can be baked into normal maps for use on lower-polygon character models in CryEngine.

Sculpting Workflow:
1. Create a high-poly character model with fine details.
2. Extract normal maps, ambient occlusion maps, and other textures.
3. Apply these textures to a low-poly character model in CryEngine for realis tic rendering.

Character Rigging and Skeletons

Character rigging involves creating a skeleton for characters and assigning controls to bones, allowing them to move and deform realistically during animation. CryEngine supports various character rigging techniques:

- **Inverse Kinematics (IK):** Implement IK chains for precise control over specific character limbs, such as arms and legs.

- **Skinning and Weight Painting:** Assign weights to vertices to control how they are influenced by nearby bones. Weight painting ensures smooth deformations.

- **Facial Rigging:** Rig the character's face to enable realistic facial expressions and animations.

Blend Shapes and Morph Targets

Blend shapes, also known as morph targets, enable character faces to express a wide range of emotions and reactions. Artists create multiple target shapes representing different facial expressions, and these targets can be blended together to create dynamic facial animations.

```
// Example code for blending morph targets in CryEngine
void BlendMorphTargets(EntityId characterEntity, const char* targetName, float weight)
{
    IEntity* pEntity = gEnv->pEntitySystem->GetEntity(characterEntity);
    if (pEntity)
    {
        // Set the weight of the specified morph target
        IMorphController* pMorphCtrl = pEntity->GetMorphController();
        pMorphCtrl->SetMorphWeightByName(targetName, weight);
    }
}
```

Realistic Hair and Fur

Creating realistic hair and fur for characters is a complex task. CryEngine offers solutions for achieving convincing hair and fur effects:

- **Hair Cards:** Use hair cards, which are flat planes with hair textures, to simulate hair and fur.

- **Hair Shaders:** Utilize specialized hair shaders in CryEngine to achieve realistic lighting and shading on character hair.

Cloth Simulation

Simulating cloth behavior adds realism to character models. CryEngine supports cloth simulation, allowing artists to create dynamic clothing and accessories for characters. Cloth can interact with the environment and respond to character movement realistically.

```
// Example code for cloth simulation in CryEngine
void SimulateCloth(EntityId characterEntity)
{
    IEntity* pEntity = gEnv->pEntitySystem->GetEntity(characterEntity);
    if (pEntity)
    {
        // Enable cloth simulation for character clothing
        IClothController* pClothCtrl = pEntity->GetClothController();
        pClothCtrl->EnableClothSimulation();
    }
}
```

LODs for Character Models

Implementing Level of Detail (LOD) for character models is crucial for optimizing performance. Create multiple LODs of character models, each with a progressively lower polygon count. CryEngine will automatically switch between LODs based on distance and screen size.

```
**LOD Guidelines:**
- Use LODs for both characters and their equipment (e.g., weapons and accesso
ries).
- Maintain consistent visual quality across LODs to ensure smooth transitions
.
- Optimize LODs for efficient rendering and reduced memory usage.
```

Animation Integration

Character models come to life through animations. CryEngine allows you to integrate animations seamlessly into your project:

- **Rigging and Animation Compatibility:** Ensure that character rigs are compatible with animation data for smooth motion.

- **Animation Blending:** Implement animation blending to create fluid transitions between different character animations, such as walking, running, and idle.

- **Blend Trees:** Utilize blend trees for complex animations, enabling characters to blend multiple animations simultaneously based on various parameters.

Performance Considerations

While striving for high-quality character models, it's essential to consider performance. Test character models on target platforms and adjust their complexity as needed to maintain smooth gameplay.

```
**Performance Optimization:**
- Use LODs effectively to reduce character polygon count at a distance.
- Minimize the number of unique characters in a scene to reduce draw calls.
- Optimize character textures and materials for efficient rendering.
```

In conclusion, advanced character modeling in CryEngine involves a combination of techniques, including polygon modeling, high-resolution sculpting, rigging, blend shapes, realistic hair and fur, cloth simulation, LODs, and animation integration. Balancing visual quality with performance optimization is essential to create compelling characters that enhance your CryEngine project's immersive experience.

4.2 High-End Rigging and Motion Capture Integration

High-quality rigging and motion capture integration are crucial elements in achieving realistic character animations in CryEngine. In this section, we will explore advanced rigging techniques and the integration of motion capture data to elevate the quality of character animations in your game project.

Advanced Rigging Techniques

Rigging for Realism

High-end rigging focuses on creating character skeletons that facilitate realistic animations. Achieving this level of realism involves the following techniques:

- **Joint Placement:** Precise placement of joints to match anatomical structures, ensuring natural deformations during animation.

- **Twist Joints:** Incorporating twist joints to improve limb deformation, especially in areas like the shoulders and thighs.

- **Control Rigs:** Implementing control rigs with intuitive manipulation handles for animators to easily pose characters.

- **Secondary Deformations:** Adding secondary deformations, such as muscle and fat simulations, to enhance realism.

```
-- Example Lua code for setting up twist joints in CryEngine
function SetupTwistJoints(characterEntity)
    local skeleton = characterEntity:GetCharacterSkeleton()

    -- Define twist joint constraints for specific bones
    skeleton:AddTwistJoint("upper_arm_L", "forearm_L", 45)
    skeleton:AddTwistJoint("upper_arm_R", "forearm_R", 45)
end
```

Facial Rigging

Facial rigging is critical for conveying emotions and expressions in characters. Achieve high-quality facial rigging through techniques such as:

- **Blend Shape Integration:** Connect blend shapes (morph targets) to facial controls to enable a wide range of facial expressions.

- **Eye Rigging:** Rigging the eyes for natural movement, including blinking, eye tracking, and squinting.

- **Lip Sync:** Implementing lip sync rigs for synchronized lip movements during dialogues.

- **Facial Capture:** Utilizing facial motion capture data for authentic expressions.

Motion Capture Integration

Motion capture (mocap) is a powerful technique for capturing real-world movements and applying them to character animations. The integration of motion capture data offers several advantages:

- **Realism:** Mocap data results in lifelike character movements, ensuring that animations look natural and convincing.

- **Time Efficiency:** Mocap accelerates animation production by providing pre-recorded motions that can be applied to characters.

- **Consistency:** Mocap ensures consistency in character movements, reducing the need for manual keyframing.

Workflow for Motion Capture Integration

Integrating motion capture data into CryEngine involves several steps:

1. **Data Acquisition:** Record motion capture data using specialized equipment and actors performing the desired actions.

2. **Data Cleaning:** Clean the captured data to remove any noise or unwanted artifacts.

3. **Character Rig Matching:** Ensure that the character rig in CryEngine matches the structure of the actors used for motion capture.

4. **Retargeting:** Apply the motion capture data to the character rig, mapping the actor's movements to the character's skeleton.

5. **Blending and Post-processing:** Blend different mocap clips together, and apply post-processing to adjust animations as needed.

6. **Integration:** Import the retargeted and processed animations into CryEngine.

```cpp
// Example C++ code for retargeting and applying mocap data in CryEngine
void ApplyMocapData(EntityId characterEntity, MocapData mocapClip)
{
    IEntity* pEntity = gEnv->pEntitySystem->GetEntity(characterEntity);
    if (pEntity)
    {
        ICharacterInstance* pCharacter = pEntity->GetCharacter(0);
        if (pCharacter)
        {
            // Apply mocap data to the character's skeleton
            pCharacter->SetMotionData(mocapClip);
        }
    }
}
```

Different motion capture technologies are available, including optical systems, inertial systems, and markerless systems. Choose the technology that suits your project's requirements and budget.

- **Optical Systems:** Use infrared cameras and reflective markers for highly accurate motion capture.

- **Inertial Systems:** Utilize sensors attached to actors' bodies to capture motion without cameras.

- **Markerless Systems:** Capture motion without markers, often using depth-sensing cameras like Kinect or structured light scanners.

Performance Optimization

While high-quality rigging and motion capture integration improve character animations, they can also impact performance. Consider the following optimization techniques:

- **LODs for Animations:** Implement level of detail (LOD) versions of animations to reduce animation complexity at a distance.

- **Animation Blending Optimization:** Optimize animation blending to minimize computational overhead.

- **Culling and LODs for Characters:** Use culling techniques and LODs for characters to reduce rendering load.

- **Streaming Animations:** Stream animations to load and unload them dynamically based on the player's location.

Testing and Fine-Tuning

Testing and fine-tuning animations are essential to ensure that character movements appear natural and glitch-free. Work closely with animators and QA teams to identify and resolve any animation issues.

In summary, advanced rigging techniques and motion capture integration in CryEngine are key to achieving realistic and high-quality character animations in your game. Rig characters with precision, employ facial rigging for expressions, and seamlessly integrate motion capture data to enhance animation realism. Remember to optimize animations and conduct thorough testing to achieve outstanding character animations that captivate players.

4.3 Complex Animation Sequences and Blending

Creating complex animation sequences and implementing blending techniques is crucial for achieving dynamic and immersive character animations in CryEngine. In this section, we will explore advanced methods for handling complex animations and seamlessly blending between them.

Animation Sequences

Layered Animation

Layered animation is a technique that involves combining multiple animation sequences on different layers to achieve complex character behaviors. In CryEngine, you can use animation layers to stack animations and control their influence on the character's movement.

```cpp
// Example C++ code for layered animation in CryEngine
void LayeredAnimation(EntityId characterEntity)
{
    IEntity* pEntity = gEnv->pEntitySystem->GetEntity(characterEntity);
    if (pEntity)
    {
        ICharacterInstance* pCharacter = pEntity->GetCharacter(0);
        if (pCharacter)
        {
            // Add a new animation layer and assign an animation sequence
            IAnimationLayerMixer* pLayerMixer = pCharacter->GetISkeletonAnim(
)->GetILayerMixer();
            int layerId = pLayerMixer->AddNewLayer();
            pLayerMixer->SetLayerPlayback(layerId, eLayerPlaybackMode::eLPM_L
ayered);
            pLayerMixer->SetLayerPlaybackWeight(layerId, 1.0f);
            pLayerMixer->SetLayerMask(layerId, "UpperBody");
            pLayerMixer->SetLayerBlendTime(layerId, 0.2f);
            pLayerMixer->SetLayerCurrentScope(layerId, "Idle");
        }
    }
}
```

Animation States and Transitions

In complex animations, characters often switch between different states, such as walking, running, and crouching. Smooth transitions between these states are essential for fluid character movement. CryEngine allows you to define animation states and set up transitions between them.

```lua
-- Example Lua code for defining animation states and transitions
local AnimationStates = {
    Idle = "Idle",
    Walk = "Walk",
```

```lua
    Run = "Run",
}

function DefineAnimationStates(characterEntity)
    local animationContext = characterEntity:GetAnimationContext()

    -- Define animation states
    animationContext:AddAnimationState(AnimationStates.Idle)
    animationContext:AddAnimationState(AnimationStates.Walk)
    animationContext:AddAnimationState(AnimationStates.Run)

    -- Set up transitions between states
    animationContext:AddTransition(AnimationStates.Idle, AnimationStates.Walk
)
    animationContext:AddTransition(AnimationStates.Walk, AnimationStates.Run)
    animationContext:AddTransition(AnimationStates.Run, AnimationStates.Walk)
end
```

Animation Blending

Blend Trees

Blend trees are a powerful tool for creating complex animations by blending multiple animation clips based on various parameters. CryEngine supports blend trees, allowing you to create intricate character animations that respond to player input and in-game conditions.

```cpp
// Example C++ code for implementing a blend tree in CryEngine
void CreateBlendTree(EntityId characterEntity)
{
    IEntity* pEntity = gEnv->pEntitySystem->GetEntity(characterEntity);
    if (pEntity)
    {
        ICharacterInstance* pCharacter = pEntity->GetCharacter(0);
        if (pCharacter)
        {
            // Create a blend tree node
            IBlendTree* pBlendTree = pCharacter->CreateBlendTree();

            // Add animation clips and define blending parameters
            pBlendTree->AddChildClip("Idle", "idle.anim");
            pBlendTree->AddChildClip("Walk", "walk.anim");
            pBlendTree->AddChildClip("Run", "run.anim");

            // Set up blending rules and transitions
            pBlendTree->SetBlendParameter("MovementSpeed");
            pBlendTree->SetBlendRule("Idle", "Walk", "MovementSpeed > 0.1");
            pBlendTree->SetBlendRule("Walk", "Run", "MovementSpeed > 1.0");
        }
```

```
        }
}
```

Inverse Kinematics (IK) Blending

IK blending allows characters to interact with the environment realistically. CryEngine supports IK blending, enabling characters to adapt their limb positions to accommodate dynamic interactions with objects, terrain, and other characters.

```cpp
// Example C++ code for IK blending in CryEngine
void ApplyIKBlending(EntityId characterEntity, Vec3 targetPosition)
{
    IEntity* pEntity = gEnv->pEntitySystem->GetEntity(characterEntity);
    if (pEntity)
    {
        ICharacterInstance* pCharacter = pEntity->GetCharacter(0);
        if (pCharacter)
        {
            // Apply IK blending to reach the target position
            IAnimationPoseBlenderDir* pPoseBlender = pCharacter->GetISkeleton
Anim()->GetIPoseBlenderAim();
            pPoseBlender->Enable(true);
            pPoseBlender->SetTarget(targetPosition);
        }
    }
}
```

Animation Events and Triggers

Animation events and triggers allow you to synchronize in-game actions with specific points in an animation sequence. These events can be used to trigger sound effects, particle effects, character abilities, and more.

```lua
-- Example Lua code for defining animation events and triggers
function DefineAnimationEvents(characterEntity)
    local animationContext = characterEntity:GetAnimationContext()

    -- Define animation events
    animationContext:AddAnimationEvent("Attack", 0.5, "OnAttackStart")
    animationContext:AddAnimationEvent("Attack", 0.8, "OnAttackEnd")

    -- Define animation triggers
    animationContext:AddAnimationTrigger("Death", 0.9, "OnCharacterDeath")
end
```

Procedural Animation

Procedural animation techniques can enhance character animations by adding realism to movements such as breathing, idling, and reacting to external forces. CryEngine supports procedural animation, allowing you to implement dynamic character behaviors.

```cpp
// Example C++ code for procedural animation in CryEngine
void ApplyProceduralAnimation(EntityId characterEntity)
{
    IEntity* pEntity = gEnv->pEntitySystem->GetEntity(characterEntity);
    if (pEntity)
    {
        ICharacterInstance* pCharacter = pEntity->GetCharacter(0);
        if (pCharacter)
        {
            // Apply procedural animation for breathing or idle movements
            IProceduralContext* pProceduralContext = pCharacter->CreateProced
uralContext();
            pProceduralContext->SetParameter("Breathing", 0.5);
        }
    }
}
```

Testing and Debugging

Thorough testing and debugging of complex animations and blending are essential to ensure that characters move naturally and respond correctly to in-game interactions. Use CryEngine's debugging tools, animation visualization, and player feedback to refine animations and transitions.

In conclusion, creating complex animation sequences and implementing blending techniques in CryEngine allows you to achieve dynamic and immersive character animations. Layered animation, animation states, blend trees, IK blending, animation events, procedural animation, and thorough testing are vital components of creating captivating character animations that enhance your game's immersion and storytelling.

4.4 Realistic Facial Animation and Emotion Capture

Realistic facial animation is essential for bringing characters to life and conveying emotions in your CryEngine project. In this section, we will explore techniques for achieving lifelike facial animations, including emotion capture and expression.

Emotion Capture

Emotion-Centric Animation

Emotion-centric animation focuses on capturing and conveying a wide range of emotions through character facial expressions. To achieve this, you can utilize emotion capture technologies, such as facial motion capture rigs, to record real emotions performed by actors.

```cpp
// Example C++ code for emotion capture integration in CryEngine
void EmotionCapture(EntityId characterEntity, Emotion emotion)
{
    IEntity* pEntity = gEnv->pEntitySystem->GetEntity(characterEntity);
    if (pEntity)
    {
        ICharacterInstance* pCharacter = pEntity->GetCharacter(0);
        if (pCharacter)
        {
            // Set the character's facial animation based on the captured emo
tion
            IFacialAnimation* pFacialAnimation = pCharacter->GetIFacialAnimat
ion();
            pFacialAnimation->PlayEmotion(emotion);
        }
    }
}
```

Blend Shapes and Morph Targets

Blend shapes, also known as morph targets, are crucial for facial animation. Create a library of blend shapes representing various facial expressions, and blend them together to create nuanced emotions.

```lua
-- Example Lua code for blend shapes in CryEngine
function BlendFacialExpressions(characterEntity, expressionWeights)
    local pEntity = gEnv.pEntitySystem:GetEntity(characterEntity)
    if pEntity then
        local pCharacter = pEntity:GetCharacter(0)
        if pCharacter then
            local pMorphCtrl = pCharacter:GetMorphController()
            for expression, weight in pairs(expressionWeights) do
                pMorphCtrl:SetMorphWeightByName(expression, weight)
            end
        end
    end
end
```

Facial Rigging and Animation

Facial Control Rigs

Facial control rigs provide animators with intuitive manipulation handles to pose character faces realistically. Implement control rigs for various facial features, such as eyebrows, lips, and eyelids, to achieve precise facial expressions.

```cpp
// Example C++ code for implementing facial control rigs in CryEngine
void CreateFacialControlRig(EntityId characterEntity)
{
    IEntity* pEntity = gEnv->pEntitySystem->GetEntity(characterEntity);
    if (pEntity)
```

```
    {
        ICharacterInstance* pCharacter = pEntity->GetCharacter(0);
        if (pCharacter)
        {
            IFacialControlRig* pFacialRig = pCharacter->CreateFacialControlRi
g();

            // Define control handles for eyebrows, lips, and eyelids
            pFacialRig->AddControl("EyebrowLeft", eFacialControlType::eFCT_Ro
tation);
            pFacialRig->AddControl("EyebrowRight", eFacialControlType::eFCT_R
otation);
            pFacialRig->AddControl("LipUpper", eFacialControlType::eFCT_Scale
);
            pFacialRig->AddControl("LipLower", eFacialControlType::eFCT_Scale
);
            pFacialRig->AddControl("EyelidUpper", eFacialControlType::eFCT_Ro
tation);
            pFacialRig->AddControl("EyelidLower", eFacialControlType::eFCT_Ro
tation);
        }
    }
}
```

Lip Sync and Speech Animation

Lip syncing is crucial for synchronized lip movements during dialogues. CryEngine supports lip sync rigs that enable characters to articulate words realistically based on audio input.

```
-- Example Lua code for lip sync in CryEngine
function ApplyLipSync(characterEntity, audioInput)
    local pEntity = gEnv.pEntitySystem:GetEntity(characterEntity)
    if pEntity then
        local pCharacter = pEntity:GetCharacter(0)
        if pCharacter then
            local pFacialAnimation = pCharacter:GetIFacialAnimation()
            pFacialAnimation:SetLipSyncInput(audioInput)
        end
    end
end
```

Expression Capture and Keyframing

Keyframing Facial Expressions

Keyframing is a traditional method of animating facial expressions by manually setting keyframes for each frame of an animation. While time-consuming, it provides precise control over character emotions.

```cpp
// Example C++ code for keyframing facial expressions in CryEngine
void KeyframeFacialExpressions(EntityId characterEntity)
{
    IEntity* pEntity = gEnv->pEntitySystem->GetEntity(characterEntity);
    if (pEntity)
    {
        ICharacterInstance* pCharacter = pEntity->GetCharacter(0);
        if (pCharacter)
        {
            IFacialAnimation* pFacialAnimation = pCharacter->GetIFacialAnimat
ion();

            // Set keyframes for various facial expressions
            pFacialAnimation->SetKeyframe("Happy", 0.0f);
            pFacialAnimation->SetKeyframe("Sad", 1.0f);
            pFacialAnimation->SetKeyframe("Angry", 2.0f);
        }
    }
}
```

Expression Capture Technologies

Expression capture technologies, such as markerless facial tracking and depth-sensing cameras, allow you to capture real-time facial expressions from actors and apply them to characters. These technologies streamline the process of achieving lifelike facial animations.

Testing and Fine-Tuning

Testing and fine-tuning facial animations are essential to ensure that character emotions are conveyed accurately. Collaborate with animators and actors to review and refine facial expressions, and use in-game feedback to make adjustments as needed.

In summary, achieving realistic facial animation and emotion capture in CryEngine is crucial for bringing characters to life

---

4.5 AI-Driven Character Behavior

AI-driven character behavior is a fundamental aspect of game development, enhancing the realism and engagement of your CryEngine project. In this section, we will delve into the intricacies of creating intelligent and adaptive non-player characters (NPCs) through advanced AI programming.

Advanced AI Programming

Behavior Trees

Behavior trees are a popular AI architecture for defining NPC behaviors. In CryEngine, you can design complex behavior trees to dictate how NPCs react to various in-game situations, making them appear more lifelike and responsive.

```lua
-- Example Lua code for defining an NPC behavior tree in CryEngine
function DefineBehaviorTree(NPCEntity)
    local behaviorTree = NPCEntity:GetBehaviorTree()

    -- Define tree nodes, tasks, and conditions
    local rootNode = behaviorTree:CreateRootNode()
    local sequenceNode = behaviorTree:CreateSequenceNode()

    local task1 = behaviorTree:CreateTask("MoveToPlayer")
    local task2 = behaviorTree:CreateTask("AttackPlayer")

    local condition1 = behaviorTree:CreateCondition("IsPlayerInRange")

    -- Construct the behavior tree
    rootNode:AddChild(sequenceNode)
    sequenceNode:AddChild(condition1)
    sequenceNode:AddChild(task1)
    sequenceNode:AddChild(task2)
end
```

State Machines

State machines are another AI architecture used to model NPC behavior. Define various states and transitions to represent different NPC behaviors and switch between them based on specific conditions or events.

```cpp
// Example C++ code for implementing an NPC state machine in CryEngine
void ImplementStateMachine(EntityId NPCEntity)
{
    IEntity* pEntity = gEnv->pEntitySystem->GetEntity(NPCEntity);
    if (pEntity)
    {
        IAIObject* pAIObject = pEntity->GetAI();
        if (pAIObject)
        {
            // Create AI states
            IAIState* pIdleState = pAIObject->CreateState("IdleState");
            IAIState* pPatrolState = pAIObject->CreateState("PatrolState");
            IAIState* pAttackState = pAIObject->CreateState("AttackState");

            // Set up state transitions
            pIdleState->AddTransition("PlayerDetected", pPatrolState);
```

```cpp
        pPatrolState->AddTransition("PlayerInRange", pAttackState);
        pAttackState->AddTransition("PlayerOutOfSight", pPatrolState);

        // Set the initial state
        pAIObject->SetCurrentState(pIdleState);
    }
  }
}
```

Adaptive NPC Behaviors

Learning Algorithms

Implement learning algorithms, such as reinforcement learning or neural networks, to enable NPCs to adapt and learn from player interactions and in-game experiences. Adaptive behaviors make NPCs more challenging and engaging.

```cpp
// Example C++ code for implementing reinforcement learning in CryEngine NPCs
void ImplementReinforcementLearning(EntityId NPCEntity)
{
    IEntity* pEntity = gEnv->pEntitySystem->GetEntity(NPCEntity);
    if (pEntity)
    {
        IAIObject* pAIObject = pEntity->GetAI();
        if (pAIObject)
        {
            // Implement reinforcement learning algorithm for NPC behavior adaptation
            // Update NPC actions based on rewards and player interactions
        }
    }
}
```

Dynamic Decision Making

Allow NPCs to make dynamic decisions by considering factors like player behavior, environmental changes, and mission objectives. Adaptive decision-making ensures that NPCs respond appropriately to evolving game scenarios.

```lua
-- Example Lua code for dynamic decision making in CryEngine NPCs
function DynamicDecisionMaking(NPCEntity, playerEntity)
    local pNPC = gEnv.pEntitySystem:GetEntity(NPCEntity)
    local pPlayer = gEnv.pEntitySystem:GetEntity(playerEntity)

    if pNPC and pPlayer then
        local distanceToPlayer = pNPC:GetWorldPos() - pPlayer:GetWorldPos()

        -- Adjust NPC behavior based on the distance to the player
        if distanceToPlayer < 10.0 then
            -- Engage in combat behavior
```

```
            pNPC:StartCombat()
        else
            -- Perform idle or patrol behavior
            pNPC:PerformIdle()
        end
    end
end
```

Efficient AI programming is crucial for maintaining game performance. Optimize AI algorithms and routines to ensure that NPCs do not cause undue strain on the game engine.

- **Pathfinding Optimization:** Use efficient pathfinding algorithms to reduce the computational load when NPCs navigate complex environments.

- **AI Culling:** Implement AI culling techniques to disable AI processing for NPCs that are far from the player's view.

- **AI LODs:** Utilize AI level of detail (LOD) techniques to simplify NPC behavior when they are not in close proximity to the player.

Testing and Debugging

Thorough testing and debugging are essential for ensuring that AI-driven character behavior is realistic, balanced, and free from glitches. Employ debugging tools and conduct playtesting to refine and fine-tune NPC behaviors.

In summary, advanced AI programming techniques in CryEngine allow you to create intelligent and adaptive NPC behaviors that enhance the immersion and challenge of your game. Implement behavior

Chapter 5: Physics and Realism

5.1 Advanced Physics Simulations in CryEngine

In the world of game development, physics simulations play a crucial role in creating immersive and realistic gameplay experiences. CryEngine offers advanced physics capabilities that enable developers to simulate a wide range of physical interactions and effects. In this section, we will explore the intricacies of implementing advanced physics simulations in CryEngine.

Utilizing CryPhysics

CryEngine leverages the CryPhysics engine, which provides a robust framework for handling physics interactions within the game world. Developers can use CryPhysics to simulate various physical phenomena, including collision detection, rigid body dynamics, and complex interactions.

```cpp
// Example C++ code for enabling CryPhysics in CryEngine
void EnableCryPhysics()
{
    if (gEnv->pPhysicsSystem)
    {
        // Initialize the CryPhysics system
        gEnv->pPhysicsSystem->Init();

        // Enable physics simulation for the game world
        gEnv->pPhysicsSystem->EnablePhysics(true);
    }
}
```

Advanced Physics Simulations

Ragdoll Physics

One of the key features of CryEngine's physics system is the support for realistic ragdoll simulations. Developers can apply ragdoll physics to characters and objects, allowing them to react dynamically to external forces and collisions.

```lua
-- Example Lua code for enabling ragdoll physics for a character in CryEngine
function EnableRagdollPhysics(characterEntity)
    local pEntity = gEnv.pEntitySystem:GetEntity(characterEntity)
    if pEntity then
        local pCharacter = pEntity:GetCharacter(0)
        if pCharacter then
            pCharacter:SetRagdollMode(1) -- Enable ragdoll physics
        end
    end
}
```

CryEngine's physics system also supports environmental destruction, allowing for dynamic destruction of objects and structures within the game world. Developers can create destructible environments by defining breakable components and setting up appropriate physics properties.

```cpp
// Example C++ code for defining a destructible object in CryEngine
void DefineDestructibleObject(EntityId destructibleEntity)
{
    IEntity* pEntity = gEnv->pEntitySystem->GetEntity(destructibleEntity);
    if (pEntity)
    {
        IPhysicalEntity* pPhysicalEntity = pEntity->GetPhysicalEntity();
        if (pPhysicalEntity)
        {
            // Define breakable properties for the physical entity
            pe_breakableparams params;
            params.nMaterial = 0; // Material index
            params.minVibrationAmt = 0.0f; // Minimum vibration amount
            params.maxVibrationAmt = 1.0f; // Maximum vibration amount
            params.fVibrationDuration = 2.0f; // Vibration duration

            // Apply the breakable properties
            pPhysicalEntity->SetParams(&params);
        }
    }
}
```

Fluid Dynamics and Interactive Elements

CryEngine supports fluid dynamics simulations, allowing developers to create realistic water and fluid interactions. Additionally, interactive elements like buoyancy and underwater physics can be implemented to enhance gameplay experiences.

```cpp
// Example C++ code for implementing fluid dynamics in CryEngine
void ImplementFluidDynamics(EntityId waterEntity)
{
    IEntity* pEntity = gEnv->pEntitySystem->GetEntity(waterEntity);
    if (pEntity)
    {
        IPhysicalEntity* pPhysicalEntity = pEntity->GetPhysicalEntity();
        if (pPhysicalEntity)
        {
            // Define fluid properties for the physical entity
            pe_params_part partParams;
            partParams.flagsAND = pef_logically_breakable;
            partParams.nMats = 1;
            partParams.pMatMapping = new pe_matid[1];
            partParams.pMatMapping[0] = 0; // Material index for water
```

```
        // Apply fluid properties to the entity
        pPhysicalEntity->SetParams(&partParams);
    }
  }
}
```

Custom Physics Solutions for Unique Gameplay

Developers often need custom physics solutions to achieve unique gameplay mechanics and effects. CryEngine's flexibility allows for the implementation of custom physics behaviors tailored to specific game requirements.

```
// Example C++ code for custom physics behavior in CryEngine
void ImplementCustomPhysics(EntityId customEntity)
{
    IEntity* pEntity = gEnv->pEntitySystem->GetEntity(customEntity);
    if (pEntity)
    {
        // Implement custom physics logic for the entity
        // This could include unique movement, collision responses, or other
physics interactions.
    }
}
```

Integrating Physics with Game Logic

Successful game development involves seamless integration of physics simulations with game logic. Developers must ensure that physics interactions influence gameplay and contribute to the overall player experience.

In conclusion, CryEngine offers advanced physics simulations that empower developers to create realistic and engaging gameplay experiences. Whether it's simulating ragdoll physics, environmental destruction, fluid dynamics, or custom physics solutions, mastering these capabilities can elevate the quality and immersion of your CryEngine project.

5.2 Creating Realistic Destruction and Environmental Effects

In the realm of game development, creating realistic destruction and environmental effects is crucial for immersing players in dynamic and engaging virtual worlds. CryEngine provides powerful tools and features for achieving lifelike destruction and environmental interactions. In this section, we will explore the techniques and capabilities that CryEngine offers for these purposes.

Dynamic Object Destruction

CryEngine allows developers to simulate dynamic object destruction realistically. Objects can be broken apart into smaller pieces, and their physical properties can change dynamically upon impact, creating a visually stunning and immersive experience.

```cpp
// Example C++ code for simulating dynamic object destruction in CryEngine
void SimulateDestruction(EntityId destructibleEntity, float impactForce)
{
    IEntity* pEntity = gEnv->pEntitySystem->GetEntity(destructibleEntity);
    if (pEntity)
    {
        IPhysicalEntity* pPhysicalEntity = pEntity->GetPhysicalEntity();
        if (pPhysicalEntity)
        {
            // Apply an external force to trigger destruction
            pe_action_impulse impulse;
            impulse.impulse = Vec3(0, 0, impactForce);
            pPhysicalEntity->Action(&impulse);
        }
    }
}
```

Particle Effects

Particle effects play a significant role in creating realistic environmental interactions. CryEngine offers a comprehensive particle system that allows developers to create a wide range of effects, including fire, smoke, debris, and explosions.

```lua
-- Example Lua code for creating a particle effect in CryEngine
function CreateParticleEffect(position, effectName)
    local particleParams = {
        position = position,
        effect = effectName,
        scale = 1.0,
        lifetime = 2.0,
        velocity = {0, 0, 0},
        rotation = {0, 0, 0},
        gravity = {0, 0, -9.81},
        wind = {0, 0, 0}
    }

    local particleId = Particle.SpawnParticle(particleParams)

    -- Attach the particle effect to a specific entity if needed
    -- Particle.AttachToEntity(particleId, entityId, ...)
end
```

Destruction Layers

CryEngine's destruction layers allow developers to define different levels of destruction for objects. These layers can be progressively destroyed, revealing new gameplay elements and altering the environment in response to player actions.

```lua
-- Example Lua code for defining destruction layers in CryEngine
function DefineDestructionLayers(destructibleEntity)
    local pEntity = gEnv.pEntitySystem:GetEntity(destructibleEntity)
    if pEntity then
        local pPhysicalEntity = pEntity:GetPhysicalEntity()
        if pPhysicalEntity then
            -- Define different destruction layers and their properties
            pPhysicalEntity:SetDestructionLayer(0, 0.2) -- Layer 0 with 20% health
            pPhysicalEntity:SetDestructionLayer(1, 0.5) -- Layer 1 with 50% health
            pPhysicalEntity:SetDestructionLayer(2, 1.0) -- Layer 2 with 100% health (indestructible)
        end
    end
}
```

Interactive Environments

CryEngine enables developers to create interactive environments where player actions have a direct impact on the surroundings. This can include destructible structures, dynamic weather systems, and responsive terrain that enhances gameplay immersion.

```cpp
// Example C++ code for creating interactive terrain in CryEngine
void CreateInteractiveTerrain()
{
    ITerrain* pTerrain = gEnv->p3DEngine->GetTerrain();
    if (pTerrain)
    {
        // Define terrain properties and parameters
        TerrainParams terrainParams;
        terrainParams.size = Vec3(512, 512, 128);
        terrainParams.resolution = 256;

        // Create interactive terrain
        pTerrain->CreateTerrain(terrainParams);
    }
}
```

Sound Effects and Audio Integration

To enhance the realism of destruction and environmental effects, audio plays a crucial role. CryEngine offers advanced audio capabilities that allow developers to integrate sound effects seamlessly with the visuals, creating a more immersive experience for players.

```lua
-- Example Lua code for playing sound effects during destruction in CryEngine
function PlayDestructionSound(position, soundName)
{
    local soundParams = {
        position = position,
        sound = soundName,
        volume = 1.0,
        pitch = 1.0,
        radius = 50.0,
        falloff = 1.0,
        doppler = 0.0
    }

    local soundId = AudioUtils.PlaySound(soundParams)
}
```

Performance Considerations

While creating realistic destruction and environmental effects is exciting, it's essential to consider performance optimization. Implement efficient culling techniques, LOD (Level of Detail) systems, and occlusion culling to ensure that the game runs smoothly without sacrificing visual quality.

In conclusion, CryEngine provides a robust set of tools and features for creating realistic destruction and environmental effects. By mastering these techniques, developers can elevate the quality of their games, immerse players in dynamic worlds, and deliver memorable gaming experiences.

5.3 Fluid Dynamics and Interactive Elements

Fluid dynamics and interactive elements play a vital role in creating realistic and engaging game environments. CryEngine provides developers with tools and features to simulate fluid behavior, water interactions, and other dynamic elements. In this section, we will explore how to leverage CryEngine's capabilities for fluid dynamics and interactive elements to enhance gameplay immersion.

Simulating Fluid Dynamics

CryEngine allows developers to simulate fluid dynamics, including water, with a high degree of realism. This capability is essential for creating visually stunning environments and enabling interactions such as swimming, splashing, and buoyancy.

```cpp
// Example C++ code for implementing fluid dynamics in CryEngine
void ImplementFluidDynamics(EntityId waterEntity)
{
    IEntity* pEntity = gEnv->pEntitySystem->GetEntity(waterEntity);
```

```
if (pEntity)
{
    IPhysicalEntity* pPhysicalEntity = pEntity->GetPhysicalEntity();
    if (pPhysicalEntity)
    {
        // Define fluid properties for the physical entity
        pe_params_part partParams;
        partParams.flagsAND = pef_logically_breakable;
        partParams.nMats = 1;
        partParams.pMatMapping = new pe_matid[1];
        partParams.pMatMapping[0] = 0; // Material index for water

        // Apply fluid properties to the entity
        pPhysicalEntity->SetParams(&partParams);
    }
}
}
```

Buoyancy and Underwater Physics

CryEngine allows developers to implement buoyancy and underwater physics, enabling objects and characters to behave realistically when submerged in water. Buoyant objects will float, while others may sink based on their properties.

```
-- Example Lua code for implementing buoyancy and underwater physics in CryEn
gine
function ImplementBuoyancy(objectEntity, waterEntity)
{
    local pObjectEntity = gEnv.pEntitySystem:GetEntity(objectEntity)
    local pWaterEntity = gEnv.pEntitySystem:GetEntity(waterEntity)

    if pObjectEntity and pWaterEntity then
        local objectPos = pObjectEntity:GetWorldPos()
        local waterPos = pWaterEntity:GetWorldPos()

        local waterLevel = waterPos.z
        local objectDepth = objectPos.z - waterLevel

        -- Apply buoyancy forces or adjust object properties based on object
depth
        if objectDepth < 0.0 then
            -- Object is underwater; apply buoyancy forces
            local buoyancyForce = Vec3(0, 0, 9.81) * pObjectEntity:GetMass()
            pObjectEntity:AddImpulse(buoyancyForce)
        else
            -- Object is above water; no buoyancy forces needed
        end
    end
}
```

Dynamic Weather Systems

CryEngine supports dynamic weather systems that can simulate various weather conditions, including rain, snow, fog, and wind. These systems can enhance gameplay by affecting visibility, physics interactions, and overall atmosphere.

```lua
-- Example Lua code for implementing dynamic weather in CryEngine
function ImplementDynamicWeather(weatherType)
{
    local weatherParams = {
        type = weatherType,
        intensity = 1.0, -- Adjust the intensity of the weather effect
        duration = 600.0, -- Set the duration of the weather effect in seconds
    }

    Weather.SetWeather(weatherParams)
}
```

Responsive Terrain

CryEngine allows developers to create responsive terrain that reacts to in-game events or player actions. This can include deformable terrain, footprints in the snow, or dynamic changes in the landscape based on scripted events.

```cpp
// Example C++ code for implementing responsive terrain in CryEngine
void CreateResponsiveTerrain(EntityId terrainEntity)
{
    ITerrain* pTerrain = gEnv->p3DEngine->GetTerrain();
    if (pTerrain)
    {
        // Define terrain properties and parameters
        TerrainParams terrainParams;
        terrainParams.size = Vec3(512, 512, 128);
        terrainParams.resolution = 256;

        // Create interactive terrain
        pTerrain->CreateTerrain(terrainParams);
    }
}
```

Integrating Audio Effects

To enhance the immersion of fluid dynamics and interactive elements, audio effects play a crucial role. CryEngine provides advanced audio capabilities, allowing developers to integrate realistic sound effects for water, weather, and interactive elements.

```lua
-- Example Lua code for playing water sound effects in CryEngine
function PlayWaterSound(position, soundName)
{
    local soundParams = {
```

```
        position = position,
        sound = soundName,
        volume = 1.0,
        pitch = 1.0,
        radius = 50.0,
        falloff = 1.0,
        doppler = 0.0
    }

    local soundId = AudioUtils.PlaySound(soundParams)
}
```

Performance Considerations

While implementing fluid dynamics and interactive elements, it's essential to consider performance optimization. Efficient culling techniques, LOD (Level of Detail) systems, and occlusion culling should be employed to maintain smooth gameplay without compromising visual quality.

In conclusion, CryEngine offers robust tools and features for simulating fluid dynamics and interactive elements, allowing developers to create immersive and dynamic game environments. By mastering these techniques, you can enhance gameplay immersion, create visually stunning scenes, and deliver memorable gaming experiences.

5.4 Custom Physics Solutions for Unique Gameplay

In game development, custom physics solutions are often necessary to achieve unique gameplay mechanics and effects that go beyond the capabilities of standard physics simulations. CryEngine's flexibility allows developers to implement custom physics behaviors tailored to specific game requirements. In this section, we will explore the concept of custom physics solutions and how to leverage CryEngine for this purpose.

Defining Custom Physics Logic

Custom physics logic involves creating unique rules and behaviors for objects, characters, or elements within the game world. This can include implementing specialized movement, collision responses, gravity effects, or any other physical interactions that are not covered by standard physics simulations.

```
// Example C++ code for implementing custom physics behavior in CryEngine
void ImplementCustomPhysics(EntityId customEntity)
{
    IEntity* pEntity = gEnv->pEntitySystem->GetEntity(customEntity);
    if (pEntity)
    {
        // Implement custom physics logic for the entity
```

```
        // This could include unique movement, collision responses, or other
physics interactions.
    }
}
```

Grappling Hooks and Unique Movement

One common use of custom physics solutions is implementing unique movement mechanics, such as grappling hooks. Developers can create custom scripts and physics interactions to simulate the behavior of grappling hooks, allowing players to swing, climb, or traverse the game world in unconventional ways.

```
-- Example Lua code for implementing a grappling hook in CryEngine
function GrapplingHook(playerEntity, targetLocation)
{
    local playerPos = playerEntity:GetWorldPos()

    -- Calculate the direction and force needed to reach the target location
    local direction = targetLocation - playerPos
    local force = direction:GetNormalized() * 1000.0

    -- Apply the force to the player character to simulate grappling
    playerEntity:AddImpulse(force)
}
```

Unique Collisions and Interactions

Custom physics solutions can be employed to define unique collision responses and interactions between objects or characters. For example, creating an object that behaves like a bouncy ball or implementing unconventional interactions between different elements in the game world.

```
// Example C++ code for creating a custom collision response in CryEngine
void CustomCollisionResponse(EntityId entityA, EntityId entityB)
{
    IEntity* pEntityA = gEnv->pEntitySystem->GetEntity(entityA);
    IEntity* pEntityB = gEnv->pEntitySystem->GetEntity(entityB);

    if (pEntityA && pEntityB)
    {
        // Implement custom collision response logic between entityA and enti
tyB
        // This could involve altering velocities, applying forces, or trigge
ring unique events.
    }
}
```

Gravity Manipulation

Custom physics solutions can also include the manipulation of gravity within the game world. Developers can script gravity changes, allowing players to experience unique gameplay scenarios, such as walking on walls or floating in zero-gravity environments.

```lua
-- Example Lua code for manipulating gravity in CryEngine
function SetCustomGravity(playerEntity, gravityDirection)
{
    local pCharacter = playerEntity:GetCharacter(0)
    if pCharacter then
        -- Set the custom gravity direction for the character
        pCharacter:SetGravity(gravityDirection)
    }
}
```

Integration with Game Logic

To ensure that custom physics solutions seamlessly integrate with game logic, developers must coordinate the timing and execution of custom physics behaviors. This involves scripting events, triggers, and conditions that trigger or control custom physics interactions based on gameplay events.

In summary, CryEngine's flexibility allows developers to implement custom physics solutions tailored to their unique gameplay ideas. Whether it's creating specialized movement mechanics, defining unique collisions, manipulating gravity, or integrating custom physics with game logic, mastering these techniques can unlock a world of creative possibilities in game development.

5.5 Integrating Physics with Game Logic

Integrating physics seamlessly with game logic is a fundamental aspect of game development. CryEngine provides powerful tools and mechanisms for developers to synchronize physics simulations with the broader gameplay experience. In this section, we will explore the importance of integrating physics with game logic and discuss various techniques for achieving this synergy.

Physics-Based Puzzles and Challenges

One common application of integrating physics with game logic is the creation of physics-based puzzles and challenges. These puzzles require players to use their understanding of in-game physics to solve problems, manipulate objects, or navigate through obstacles.

```cpp
// Example C++ code for a physics-based puzzle in CryEngine
void PhysicsBasedPuzzle(EntityId puzzleObject, bool isSolved)
{
```

```cpp
IEntity* pPuzzleObject = gEnv->pEntitySystem->GetEntity(puzzleObject);
if (pPuzzleObject)
{
    if (isSolved)
    {
        // Modify the puzzle object's properties or behavior
        // This could involve changing its physical state, appearance, or
interactions.
    }
    else
    {
        // Reset the puzzle object to its initial state
        // Ensure that any physics-related changes are reversed.
    }
}
}
```

Realistic Vehicle Physics

For games that involve vehicles, integrating realistic vehicle physics with game logic is crucial. CryEngine provides a vehicle physics system that allows developers to create vehicles with authentic handling characteristics, suspension dynamics, and collision behaviors.

```lua
-- Example Lua code for integrating vehicle physics in CryEngine
function CreateVehicle(entityId, vehicleType)
{
    local vehicleParams = {
        entityId = entityId,
        vehicleType = vehicleType,
        autoStart = true,
        physics = {
            enginePower = 500,    -- Adjust engine power
            suspensionStiffness = 5.0,   -- Adjust suspension stiffness
            -- Other vehicle physics parameters
        },
        -- Other vehicle settings
    }

    Vehicle.Spawn(vehicleParams)
}
```

Ragdoll Physics and Character Animation

Integrating ragdoll physics with character animation is essential for creating realistic character behaviors and responses to in-game events. CryEngine allows developers to blend character animations seamlessly with ragdoll physics when characters are subjected to external forces or collisions.

```cpp
// Example C++ code for integrating ragdoll physics with character animation
in CryEngine
void ApplyRagdollPhysics(EntityId characterEntity, bool enableRagdoll)
{
    IEntity* pCharacterEntity = gEnv->pEntitySystem->GetEntity(characterEntit
y);
    if (pCharacterEntity)
    {
        ICharacterInstance* pCharacterInstance = pCharacterEntity->GetCharact
er(0);
        if (pCharacterInstance)
        {
            // Enable or disable ragdoll physics based on gameplay events
            pCharacterInstance->EnableRagdollPhysics(enableRagdoll);

            if (enableRagdoll)
            {
                // Apply external forces or events to trigger ragdoll physics
                // This can be used for character knockback, explosions, or o
ther physical interactions.
            }
        }
    }
}
```

Physics-Driven Events and Triggers

Integrating physics-driven events and triggers allows for dynamic and interactive
gameplay experiences. Developers can create scripted events that respond to physics
interactions, such as triggering the collapse of a bridge when a specific load is applied or
simulating a domino effect.

```lua
-- Example Lua code for a physics-driven event trigger in CryEngine
function PhysicsEventTrigger(entityA, entityB)
{
    local pEntityA = gEnv.pEntitySystem:GetEntity(entityA)
    local pEntityB = gEnv.pEntitySystem:GetEntity(entityB)

    if pEntityA and pEntityB then
        -- Implement custom logic based on the collision or interaction betwe
en entityA and entityB
        -- This could involve triggering scripted events, altering gameplay p
arameters, or creating unique in-game situations.
    }
}
```

Feedback and Immersion

Integrating physics with game logic also plays a significant role in providing feedback and
enhancing immersion. Whether it's the tactile feel of a character's movement, the

responsiveness of in-game objects, or the realism of environmental interactions, physics integration contributes to a more engaging gaming experience.

In conclusion, integrating physics with game logic is an essential aspect of creating immersive and dynamic gameplay in CryEngine. Developers can leverage physics-based puzzles, realistic vehicle handling, character animation, scripted events, and more to craft memorable gaming experiences that engage players on a physical and emotional level.

Chapter 6: Immersive Audio Design

6.1. Advanced Techniques in Sound Design and Scoring

In the world of game development, audio plays a crucial role in creating immersive and engaging experiences for players. Advanced sound design and scoring techniques can elevate a game's audio to new heights, enhancing the overall player experience. This section explores various advanced techniques that game developers can employ to achieve immersive audio design and scoring.

The Role of Sound Design

Sound design is the art of creating and manipulating audio elements to complement the visual aspects of a game. It involves the creation of sound effects, ambiances, and Foley sounds that enrich the game world. Advanced sound design goes beyond basic audio cues and involves a deep understanding of how sound can convey emotions, enhance storytelling, and provide important gameplay feedback.

In advanced sound design, attention to detail is paramount. Game developers must consider not only what the player hears but also how they hear it. This involves the use of spatial audio techniques, dynamic audio systems, and adaptive soundscapes that respond to player actions and the game environment.

Spatial Audio and Acoustic Modeling

Spatial audio is a key component of immersive sound design. It simulates the way sound propagates in the real world, taking into account factors like distance, direction, and occlusion. With the advancement of technology, developers can now implement 3D audio and acoustic modeling to create lifelike audio experiences.

Implementing spatial audio requires careful consideration of the game's audio engine and the use of techniques such as ray tracing for audio, binaural audio rendering, and HRTF (Head-Related Transfer Function) simulations. These techniques enable players to perceive sound sources as if they were coming from specific directions and distances, adding a layer of realism to the audio.

Interactive Music and Adaptive Soundtracks

Traditional linear soundtracks have their place in gaming, but advanced techniques involve interactive and adaptive music systems. These systems respond to the player's actions, dynamically changing the music to match the on-screen events and player choices. Adaptive soundtracks create a seamless and personalized audio experience, enhancing immersion.

Developers can use middleware and audio engines that support dynamic music composition and branching audio. By integrating these systems, games can transition between different musical themes, intensify the music during action sequences, and create emotional resonance by aligning the soundtrack with the narrative.

Voice Acting and Dialogue Implementation

Voice acting plays a vital role in bringing game characters to life. In advanced audio design, hiring skilled voice actors and actresses is crucial for delivering authentic performances. Additionally, the implementation of dialogue systems that handle branching conversations and player choices adds depth to character interactions.

Developers must consider lip synchronization, emotional expression, and localization when implementing voice acting. Advanced dialogue systems may use natural language processing to allow for more natural player interactions and responses from non-player characters (NPCs).

Audio Optimization for Different Platforms

As games are often played on various platforms, audio optimization is essential to ensure a consistent and high-quality audio experience across different devices. Advanced audio design involves creating adaptive audio assets and employing compression techniques to minimize storage and memory usage while maintaining audio fidelity.

Furthermore, developers should consider platform-specific audio APIs and hardware capabilities to harness the full potential of each platform. This includes optimizing audio for consoles, PC, mobile devices, and VR/AR headsets, ensuring that the audio adapts seamlessly to each platform's requirements.

In conclusion, advanced sound design and scoring techniques are integral to creating immersive and memorable gaming experiences. Game developers should strive to push the boundaries of audio design, leveraging spatial audio, adaptive soundtracks, voice acting, and optimization to craft audio experiences that captivate players and enhance the overall gameplay. By mastering these techniques, developers can elevate their games to new levels of immersion and engagement.

6.2. 3D Spatial Audio and Acoustic Modeling

In the realm of immersive audio design, 3D spatial audio and acoustic modeling take center stage. These techniques play a pivotal role in creating lifelike and captivating soundscapes that enhance the overall gaming experience.

Understanding Spatial Audio

Spatial audio is the art of reproducing sound in a three-dimensional space, replicating the way we hear sounds in the real world. In games, this means that audio sources are positioned within the virtual environment, allowing players to perceive sound as coming from specific directions and distances. This spatial awareness adds a layer of realism and immersion to the game world.

Techniques for Implementing Spatial Audio

To implement spatial audio effectively, developers need to consider several techniques:

1. **HRTF (Head-Related Transfer Function)**: HRTF is a mathematical model used to simulate how sound waves interact with the listener's head and ears. By applying HRTF filters to audio sources, developers can create the illusion of 3D sound. This technique is essential for making sounds appear to come from different angles and elevations.

2. **Binaural Audio**: Binaural audio recordings and processing mimic the human hearing process by capturing sound with two microphones placed in the same positions as the human ears. When played back through headphones, binaural audio provides an incredibly realistic and immersive experience, making players feel like they're inside the game world.

3. **Real-time Ray Tracing**: Modern gaming engines and audio middleware support real-time ray tracing for audio. This technique traces the paths of sound rays as they interact with the virtual environment, including objects, walls, and obstacles. By accurately modeling sound propagation, ray tracing ensures that audio reflects the virtual world's geometry realistically.

4. **Sound Occlusion and Reflection**: Implementing occlusion and reflection effects is essential for creating a convincing 3D audio experience. When a sound source is blocked by an object or reflects off surfaces, players should hear the corresponding changes in audio. This adds depth to the game world and helps players locate sound sources accurately.

Benefits of 3D Spatial Audio

Implementing 3D spatial audio and acoustic modeling offers several key benefits:

- **Realism**: Players can better perceive the game world, immersing themselves in a truly three-dimensional auditory environment. This heightened realism enhances the overall gaming experience and emotional engagement.

- **Improved Gameplay**: Spatial audio can be used strategically to provide important gameplay cues. For example, players can detect enemy positions, approaching threats, or hidden items based on sound alone, enriching gameplay depth and strategy.

- **Narrative Enhancement**: Spatial audio can convey storytelling elements by immersing players in the game world. For instance, ambient sounds, whispers, or distant conversations can add depth to the narrative and create a more immersive storytelling experience.

- **Increased Immersion**: The ability to pinpoint sound sources enhances immersion. Players can instinctively react to auditory cues, making them feel more connected to the virtual environment and its inhabitants.

- **Compatibility**: Most gaming platforms and hardware support spatial audio technologies, making it accessible to a broad audience. From high-end gaming rigs to mobile devices and VR headsets, players can enjoy the benefits of 3D spatial audio.

In summary, 3D spatial audio and acoustic modeling are essential tools in a game developer's arsenal for creating immersive and captivating audio experiences. By understanding and implementing these techniques, developers can transport players into rich and convincing game worlds where sound enhances their perception and interaction with the virtual environment.

6.3. Interactive Music and Adaptive Soundtracks

One of the cornerstones of advanced audio design in modern games is the implementation of interactive music and adaptive soundtracks. These techniques allow developers to create dynamic and responsive audio experiences that adapt to the player's actions, enhancing immersion and emotional engagement.

The Role of Interactive Music

Interactive music refers to a system where the game's soundtrack reacts to in-game events, player actions, or changes in the game's pacing. Unlike traditional linear music tracks, interactive music is composed of individual segments or layers that can be triggered or modified in real-time. This dynamic approach ensures that the music remains synchronized with the gameplay, creating a seamless and personalized audio experience.

Key Elements of Interactive Music

To implement interactive music effectively, game developers need to consider several key elements:

1. **Music Segmentation**: Interactive music is composed of segmented pieces, allowing the game to play, stop, or transition between different parts of the soundtrack based on predefined conditions. Segmentation enables the music to adapt to changes in the game environment or narrative.

2. **Stingers and Transitions**: Stingers are short musical cues or effects that punctuate specific in-game events or actions. Transitions smoothly shift the music between different segments, ensuring that the changes are seamless and not jarring to the player.

3. **Layered Music**: Layering involves playing multiple musical layers simultaneously, with each layer representing a different instrument or mood. The game can adjust the volume or intensity of these layers dynamically to match the current situation, creating a rich and evolving sonic landscape.

4. **Dynamic Crossfading**: Crossfading allows for gradual transitions between different musical segments or layers. It prevents abrupt shifts in the music, making the changes less noticeable to the player.

Benefits of Adaptive Soundtracks

The implementation of adaptive soundtracks offers several notable benefits in game design:

- **Enhanced Immersion**: Adaptive soundtracks can heighten immersion by responding to the player's actions and the game's narrative. For example, the music can become more intense during combat sequences or shift to a melancholic theme during emotional moments.

- **Player Engagement**: Interactive music can help maintain player engagement by providing audio cues and feedback. For instance, a change in music can indicate the successful completion of a puzzle or the presence of hidden secrets.

- **Emotional Impact**: Adaptive soundtracks can significantly enhance the emotional impact of a game. By aligning the music with the story's emotional beats, developers can evoke a deeper emotional response from players.

- **Gameplay Variety**: Dynamic music systems add variety to gameplay experiences. Players are less likely to grow tired of repetitive music, as the soundtrack evolves with the gameplay.

- **Narrative Integration**: Interactive music can seamlessly integrate with the game's narrative, amplifying storytelling elements and player immersion. For example, a character's leitmotif can be dynamically woven into the music when that character is on screen.

In conclusion, interactive music and adaptive soundtracks are powerful tools that can elevate a game's audio to new heights. By embracing these techniques, game developers can create audio experiences that are not only engaging but also responsive to player actions, enriching the overall gaming experience. The synergy between adaptive soundtracks and gameplay creates a dynamic and immersive auditory journey that keeps players deeply engaged in the virtual worlds they explore.

6.4. Voice Acting and Dialogue Implementation

Voice acting and dialogue implementation are essential components of immersive audio design in video games. High-quality voiceovers, well-crafted scripts, and effective dialogue systems can significantly enhance the storytelling and character development aspects of a game.

The Importance of Voice Acting

Voice acting brings characters to life by giving them voices, personalities, and emotional depth. Well-executed voice acting can establish a strong connection between players and the game's characters, making the narrative more engaging and memorable. Here are some key aspects to consider:

Casting and Direction

Selecting the right voice actors for each character is crucial. Casting decisions should align with the character's personality, age, gender, and emotional range. Effective direction during recording sessions ensures that voice actors deliver performances that match the game's tone and narrative.

Script Writing

Dialogue writing is an art in itself. Game writers must craft compelling and believable dialogue that fits the characters and story. Effective dialogue enhances character development, provides context, and drives the plot forward.

Emotional Impact

Voice acting can evoke powerful emotions in players. A talented voice actor can convey a character's happiness, sadness, anger, or fear, making players empathize with the in-game personas. Emotional resonance adds depth to the gaming experience.

Dialogue Implementation

Implementing dialogue effectively within a game requires a robust system to manage character interactions, branching narratives, and player choices. Dialogue systems come in various forms, including:

Linear Dialogue

In linear dialogue systems, conversations follow a predetermined script without player input. This is common in story-driven games where the narrative is tightly controlled.

Branching Dialogue

Branching dialogue allows player choices to influence the direction of the conversation and the game's outcome. Choices can lead to different story paths, character relationships, or consequences.

Dynamic Dialogue

Dynamic dialogue adapts to the game's context and player actions. NPCs may comment on the player's achievements, current location, or decisions, making the world feel alive and responsive.

Voice Synthesis

Some games use voice synthesis technology to generate character voices in real-time. While not as common as pre-recorded voice acting, voice synthesis can provide unique opportunities for player customization and dynamic storytelling.

Benefits of Effective Voice Acting and Dialogue

High-quality voice acting and well-implemented dialogue systems offer several advantages:

- **Enhanced Immersion**: Voice acting adds depth and personality to characters, making the game world feel more immersive and believable.

- **Engaging Storytelling**: Effective dialogue can captivate players, driving them to explore the narrative and become emotionally invested in the game's events.

- **Player Agency**: Branching dialogue systems empower players to shape the story, encouraging replayability and a sense of agency.

- **Character Development**: Voice acting allows for nuanced performances that contribute to character development and player attachment to in-game personas.

- **Memorable Moments**: Memorable lines and performances can create iconic moments that players remember long after completing the game.

In conclusion, voice acting and dialogue implementation are integral to creating compelling and emotionally resonant gaming experiences. These aspects contribute to character depth, storytelling quality, and player engagement. When executed effectively, voice acting and dialogue systems enrich the audio landscape of a game and elevate it to new heights of immersion and storytelling prowess.

6.5. Audio Optimization for Different Platforms

Audio optimization is a critical aspect of game development, ensuring that the audio experience remains consistent and high-quality across various gaming platforms. Different platforms, such as PC, consoles, and mobile devices, have varying hardware capabilities and limitations. To deliver a seamless audio experience, developers must optimize audio assets, codecs, and playback systems for each platform. Here's a closer look at the importance of audio optimization for different platforms and some best practices:

Platform-Specific Challenges

Each gaming platform presents unique challenges and opportunities for audio optimization:

PC Gaming

- **Diverse Hardware**: PCs come in various configurations, making it challenging to predict the available processing power and audio capabilities of the player's system.
- **Customization**: PC gamers often have control over audio settings, requiring games to adapt to user preferences and hardware configurations.

Console Gaming

- **Fixed Hardware**: Consoles have consistent hardware specifications, allowing developers to optimize audio specifically for the platform.
- **Performance Constraints**: While console hardware is fixed, it still has performance constraints that developers must consider, especially in demanding games.

Mobile Gaming

- **Limited Resources**: Mobile devices have limited processing power and memory, making it crucial to optimize audio assets for minimal resource usage.
- **Battery Life**: Audio playback can impact battery life, so efficient audio optimization can help extend gameplay on mobile devices.

Best Practices for Audio Optimization

To ensure that audio performs well across different platforms, developers should follow these best practices:

Asset Compression

- Compress audio assets using suitable codecs (e.g., AAC, MP3, or Ogg Vorbis) to reduce file sizes without sacrificing quality.
- Utilize platform-specific compression options or tools to ensure compatibility and efficiency.

Dynamic Quality Adjustments

- Implement dynamic audio quality adjustments based on the platform's capabilities and available resources.
- For example, reduce the number of simultaneous sound sources or lower audio quality settings on less powerful devices.

Streamlining Audio Logic

- Optimize audio logic to minimize CPU and memory usage. Use efficient algorithms and data structures for audio processing.
- Implement audio occlusion and attenuation systems to reduce the processing load when sounds are not in the player's vicinity.

Audio Resource Management

- Load and unload audio assets efficiently during gameplay to conserve memory resources.
- Implement streaming for large audio files or background music to minimize memory usage.

Platform-Specific Features

- Leverage platform-specific audio features and APIs for enhanced audio experiences. This can include hardware-accelerated audio effects or surround sound support.
- Ensure compatibility with platform-specific audio requirements and standards.

Testing and Profiling

- Regularly test and profile audio performance on different platforms to identify bottlenecks or issues.
- Use profiling tools provided by platform SDKs to optimize audio code and assets.

Player Control

- Provide in-game audio settings that allow players to customize audio options, including volume levels, quality settings, and speaker configurations.

Conclusion

Audio optimization for different gaming platforms is essential to deliver a consistent and enjoyable audio experience to players. By considering platform-specific challenges and following best practices, game developers can ensure that their games sound great on a wide range of devices, enhancing player immersion and satisfaction. Effective audio optimization is a crucial part of the overall game development process and contributes to the success of a game across multiple platforms.

Chapter 7: Next-Level AI and NPC Interaction

7.1. Crafting Complex AI Behaviors and Patterns

Crafting complex AI behaviors and patterns is a fundamental aspect of modern game development, as it significantly impacts gameplay, immersion, and player engagement. In this section, we will delve into the intricacies of designing advanced AI systems that can adapt, learn, and interact with the game world and players in sophisticated ways.

The Evolution of AI in Games

Over the years, AI in games has evolved from simple scripted behaviors to dynamic and responsive systems. Today, players expect AI characters to exhibit lifelike behaviors, make intelligent decisions, and react realistically to the game environment. Achieving this level of complexity requires a combination of techniques and technologies.

Key Components of Advanced AI

Decision-Making Algorithms

Advanced AI relies on decision-making algorithms that take into account various factors, such as player actions, environmental conditions, and the AI's own objectives. Machine learning and probabilistic reasoning are often used to create decision models that mimic human-like choices.

State Machines

State machines are essential tools for defining AI behaviors. They allow AI characters to transition between different states based on events and conditions. By designing well-structured state machines, developers can create intricate patterns of behavior.

Learning and Adaptation

Modern AI systems can learn and adapt over time. Machine learning algorithms, reinforcement learning, and neural networks enable AI to improve their performance through experience. This results in AI characters that become more challenging as players progress.

Environmental Awareness

Advanced AI is aware of its surroundings. It can perceive the game world, including objects, obstacles, and other characters, and react accordingly. Spatial awareness and pathfinding algorithms are crucial for creating believable AI navigation.

Natural Language Processing (NLP)

In games with dialogue systems, NLP enables AI characters to understand and generate natural language. This is especially important for interactive storytelling and branching narratives.

Designing Complex AI Behaviors

Creating complex AI behaviors requires a thoughtful design process:

Define Objectives

Start by defining the AI's objectives and goals. What should the AI character achieve within the game? Understanding its purpose helps shape its behavior.

Analyze Player Interactions

Consider how players will interact with the AI. What actions can players take, and how should the AI respond to each of them? Account for different playstyles and strategies.

Balance Challenge and Fairness

AI should provide a challenging experience without becoming frustratingly difficult. Striking the right balance between challenge and fairness is crucial for player enjoyment.

Iterative Development

Developing AI behaviors is an iterative process. Test and refine the AI continuously, considering player feedback and adjusting behavior patterns as needed.

Player Feedback

Collect feedback from playtesters to gauge the effectiveness of AI behaviors. Use this feedback to make improvements and fine-tune the AI's responses.

Advanced AI in Different Game Genres

AI behaviors can vary significantly depending on the game genre:

- **Action Games**: AI in action games often focuses on combat tactics, enemy coordination, and cover-based strategies.
- **Role-Playing Games (RPGs)**: In RPGs, AI may emphasize character interactions, quest decisions, and dialogues.
- **Strategy Games**: AI in strategy games needs to manage resources, plan strategic moves, and adapt to changing game conditions.

Conclusion

Crafting complex AI behaviors and patterns is an essential aspect of modern game development. It involves a combination of decision-making algorithms, state machines, learning, environmental awareness, and natural language processing. By designing AI that can adapt, interact, and challenge players in sophisticated ways, developers can enhance the overall gaming experience and create more immersive and engaging worlds for players to explore.

7.2. Dynamic NPC Interactions and Story Integration

Dynamic NPC interactions and story integration are critical elements of creating immersive and engaging gameplay experiences. In this section, we will explore the intricacies of designing non-player characters (NPCs) that can adapt to player choices and contribute to a dynamic narrative.

The Role of NPCs in Games

NPCs play various roles in games, from quest givers and merchants to enemies and companions. They serve as a means to advance the storyline, provide information, and offer challenges to players. Dynamic NPC interactions enhance the player's sense of agency within the game world.

Designing Dynamic Dialogue Systems

Dynamic dialogue systems allow NPCs to respond to player choices and actions. Here are key considerations for designing such systems:

Branching Narratives

Branching narratives offer players choices that impact the storyline. Each choice leads to different consequences and outcomes. Designing branching narratives requires careful planning to ensure coherence and consistency.

Player-Driven Conversations

Allow players to initiate and control conversations with NPCs. This empowers players to explore the narrative at their own pace and dig deeper into the game world's lore.

Relationship Systems

Implementing relationship systems between NPCs and the player character can add depth to interactions. NPCs may react differently based on the player's reputation, choices, and previous interactions.

Contextual Responses

Ensure that NPC responses are contextually relevant. NPCs should acknowledge the player's progress, achievements, and previous conversations, creating a sense of continuity and immersion.

Emergent Gameplay

Dynamic NPC interactions can lead to emergent gameplay moments where unexpected events unfold based on player choices. These moments contribute to the uniqueness of each player's experience.

Technical Implementation

Implementing dynamic NPC interactions requires a combination of scripting, branching dialogue trees, and event triggers. Here's a simplified example in pseudocode:

```
# Define an NPC character
npc = NPC("John")

# Create a dialogue tree
dialogue_tree = DialogueTree()

# Define dialogue options and responses
option1 = DialogueOption("Ask about a quest")
response1 = DialogueResponse("Certainly! We have a problem with goblins in th
e nearby forest. Will you help?")
option2 = DialogueOption("Inquire about rumors")
response2 = DialogueResponse("I've heard rumors of treasure hidden in the old
ruins. Would you like to explore them?")
option3 = DialogueOption("Say goodbye")
response3 = DialogueResponse("Goodbye!")

# Connect options and responses in the dialogue tree
dialogue_tree.add_option(option1, response1)
dialogue_tree.add_option(option2, response2)
dialogue_tree.add_option(option3, response3)

# Start a conversation with the player
npc.start_dialogue(dialogue_tree)

# Based on the player's choice, trigger events or update the game state
if player_choice == "Ask about a quest":
    start_quest()
elif player_choice == "Inquire about rumors":
    explore_ruins()
else:
    end_conversation()
```

Balancing Player Freedom and Narrative Cohesion

While dynamic NPC interactions offer player agency, it's essential to balance freedom with narrative cohesion. Design choices should ensure that the storyline remains coherent and that player choices have meaningful consequences.

Conclusion

Dynamic NPC interactions and story integration are essential for creating immersive and player-driven experiences in games. By designing dialogue systems, relationship mechanics, and emergent gameplay opportunities, developers can enhance the depth of interaction between players and NPCs, making the game world more engaging and memorable.

7.3. Advanced Pathfinding and Navigation Systems

Advanced pathfinding and navigation systems are crucial components of modern game development, especially when it comes to creating intelligent and immersive NPCs. In this section, we'll delve into the intricacies of designing and implementing sophisticated pathfinding and navigation systems that enhance the behavior of NPCs in your game world.

The Importance of Pathfinding

Pathfinding is the process by which NPCs and entities in a game find the optimal path from one location to another while avoiding obstacles and obstructions. It plays a vital role in various aspects of game development, including AI, level design, and gameplay.

Key Applications of Pathfinding:

1. **NPC Movement:** Pathfinding enables NPCs to navigate through complex environments, following player characters, and responding to dynamic changes in the game world.

2. **Enemy Behavior:** Enemies can use pathfinding to track and pursue the player, creating challenging encounters and ambushes.

3. **Player Companion AI:** Companions or allies of the player character can use pathfinding to follow the player intelligently, avoid getting stuck, and participate effectively in combat and exploration.

Navigation Meshes

One of the fundamental components of advanced pathfinding systems is the navigation mesh. A navigation mesh is a simplified representation of the game world, consisting of polygons that describe walkable areas. NPCs use these polygons to plan their routes efficiently.

Benefits of Navigation Meshes:

- Reduced computational complexity: Pathfinding on a navigation mesh is faster and less resource-intensive compared to grid-based approaches.
- Realistic NPC movement: NPCs can navigate smoothly around obstacles and make decisions based on the terrain's shape.

- Dynamic updates: Navigation meshes can be updated dynamically to reflect changes in the game world, such as destructible terrain or moving platforms.

Various pathfinding algorithms are used in game development, each with its strengths and weaknesses. Some of the commonly used algorithms include:

- _A_ (A-Star):_* A* is a popular choice due to its efficiency and ability to find optimal paths. It uses heuristics to guide the search process.

- **Dijkstra's Algorithm:** While not as efficient as A*, Dijkstra's algorithm guarantees finding the shortest path, making it suitable for certain game scenarios.

- **Navigation Mesh-based Algorithms:** Specialized algorithms tailored for navigation meshes, like Recast/Detour, are efficient for complex 3D environments.

In addition to pathfinding, local avoidance and crowd simulation are essential for creating believable NPC behaviors in crowded or dynamic environments. These techniques ensure that NPCs can navigate around each other without colliding.

Local Avoidance Techniques:
- **Steering Behaviors:** NPCs apply steering behaviors like separation, alignment, and cohesion to avoid collisions and maintain group formations.

- **Reciprocal Velocity Obstacles (RVO):** RVO algorithms calculate collision-free velocities for each NPC based on their predicted movements.

Here's a simplified example of using the A* algorithm in pseudocode:

```
# Initialize the open list with the starting node
open_list = [start_node]

# Initialize the closed list as empty
closed_list = []

while open_list is not empty:
    # Select the node with the lowest cost from the open list
    current_node = select_node_with_lowest_cost(open_list)

    # Move the current node from the open list to the closed list
    open_list.remove(current_node)
    closed_list.append(current_node)

    # If the current node is the goal, path found
    if current_node == goal_node:
```

```
        return reconstruct_path(goal_node)

    # Generate successor nodes and calculate their costs
    successors = generate_successor_nodes(current_node)
    for successor in successors:
        if successor in closed_list:
            continue  # Skip nodes in the closed list
        if successor not in open_list:
            open_list.append(successor)  # Add new nodes to the open list

# No path found
return None
```

Conclusion

Advanced pathfinding and navigation systems are integral to creating engaging and lifelike NPC behaviors in games. By understanding the principles of navigation meshes, selecting appropriate pathfinding algorithms, and incorporating local avoidance techniques, developers can ensure that NPCs move intelligently and realistically within the game world, enhancing the overall gaming experience.

7.4. AI in Multiplayer: Balancing and Design Strategies

Integrating artificial intelligence (AI) into multiplayer games poses unique challenges and opportunities. In this section, we will explore the complexities of designing AI systems for multiplayer environments and discuss strategies for achieving balance and engaging gameplay.

The Role of AI in Multiplayer Games

AI in multiplayer games serves several essential functions:

1. **Non-Player Characters (NPCs):** AI-controlled NPCs can enhance the game's immersion by populating the game world with diverse characters and providing players with challenges and objectives.

2. **Bot Players:** AI bots can fill empty slots in multiplayer matches, ensuring that games remain engaging even when there aren't enough human players.

3. **Balancing:** AI can be used to balance teams in asymmetric multiplayer games, ensuring that matches are fair and enjoyable for all players.

Design Considerations

Skill Levels and Adaptability:

AI in multiplayer games should exhibit different skill levels to accommodate players of varying abilities. This can be achieved by adjusting parameters such as reaction times, accuracy, and decision-making.

Additionally, AI should adapt to the gameplay environment. For example, in team-based games, AI should be aware of the team's overall strategy and adapt its behavior accordingly.

Fairness and Challenge:

Balancing AI to provide an appropriate level of challenge is crucial. AI should be challenging but not unbeatable, ensuring that players feel a sense of accomplishment when they win.

To achieve this, designers can implement dynamic difficulty adjustment (DDA), where AI adapts its skill based on the player's performance. This ensures that skilled players face tougher AI opponents while newer players face more forgiving AI.

Player Interaction:

Multiplayer AI should interact with human players in a believable and engaging manner. This includes using communication systems, responding to player actions, and coordinating with teammates.

Team Dynamics:

In team-based multiplayer games, AI should understand the importance of teamwork. This involves coordinating attacks, defending objectives, and adapting to the team's strategy.

AI in Asymmetric Multiplayer

Asymmetric multiplayer games, where teams have different abilities or objectives, present unique challenges for AI design. In such games, AI should ensure balance and fairness.

Designers can use AI to bolster the weaker team by providing them with AI-controlled characters or advantages. Alternatively, AI can serve as a challenging adversary for the stronger team, adding depth to the gameplay.

Code Example: Dynamic Difficulty Adjustment

```python
class MultiplayerAI:
    def __init__(self, skill_level):
        self.skill_level = skill_level
        self.adjust_skill()

    def adjust_skill(self):
        # Implement dynamic difficulty adjustment based on player performance
```

```python
        if self.skill_level == "easy":
            self.accuracy = 0.6
        elif self.skill_level == "medium":
            self.accuracy = 0.7
        elif self.skill_level == "hard":
            self.accuracy = 0.8

    def update(self, player_performance):
        # Adjust AI behavior based on player's performance
        if player_performance == "poor":
            self.skill_level = "easy"
        elif player_performance == "average":
            self.skill_level = "medium"
        elif player_performance == "skilled":
            self.skill_level = "hard"

        self.adjust_skill()
```

Conclusion

Integrating AI into multiplayer games requires careful design and consideration of various factors, including skill levels, fairness, player interaction, and team dynamics. By implementing adaptable and balanced AI systems, developers can create engaging and competitive multiplayer experiences that cater to a wide range of players. Additionally, dynamic difficulty adjustment can enhance player engagement by tailoring the AI's challenge level to individual player performance.

7.5. Procedural Content Generation with AI

Procedural content generation (PCG) is a powerful technique used in game development to create vast and diverse game worlds, levels, and content. When combined with AI, PCG can offer a dynamic and ever-evolving gaming experience. In this section, we'll explore the concept of procedural content generation with AI and its applications.

What is Procedural Content Generation?

Procedural content generation refers to the creation of in-game content algorithmically rather than manually. This content can include terrain, level layouts, textures, character attributes, and even narrative elements. The goal is to generate content that feels both random and purposeful, enhancing replayability and player engagement.

AI in Procedural Content Generation

AI plays a pivotal role in procedural content generation by making content creation more intelligent, adaptive, and responsive to player actions. Here are some key areas where AI is applied:

1. Terrain Generation:

AI algorithms can create realistic and varied terrains, adapting to factors like climate, geography, and player exploration patterns. This leads to more immersive open-world environments.

2. Level Design:

AI-driven level generators can create challenging and balanced levels by analyzing player skill and preferences. This ensures that levels remain engaging and suitable for players of all skill levels.

3. Storytelling:

AI can craft dynamic narratives by considering player choices and actions, resulting in branching storylines and unique experiences for each player.

4. Enemy Behavior:

AI-controlled enemies can adapt their strategies based on the player's actions, creating a more challenging and unpredictable gameplay experience.

5. Item Placement:

AI algorithms can intelligently place items, weapons, and power-ups in the game world, optimizing player progression and balance.

6. Player Personalization:

By analyzing player behavior and preferences, AI can generate content tailored to individual players, enhancing player satisfaction and engagement.

Code Example: Procedural Terrain Generation

```python
class ProceduralTerrainGenerator:
    def __init__(self, seed):
        self.seed = seed

    def generate_terrain(self, size):
        # Implement terrain generation algorithm based on seed and size
        terrain_data = []

        # Generate terrain data here...

        return terrain_data

    def apply_texture(self, terrain_data):
        # Apply textures based on terrain data
        textured_terrain = []

        # Apply textures here...
```

```
    return textured_terrain
```

```
terrain_generator = ProceduralTerrainGenerator(seed=123)
terrain_data = terrain_generator.generate_terrain(size=(512, 512))
textured_terrain = terrain_generator.apply_texture(terrain_data)
```

Benefits of Procedural Content Generation with AI

1. **Infinite Variety:** PCG with AI can create an endless variety of content, ensuring that players never experience the same game twice.

2. **Efficiency:** It reduces the need for manual content creation, saving development time and resources.

3. **Adaptability:** AI-driven PCG can respond to player actions and preferences, creating a more personalized gaming experience.

4. **Replayability:** Dynamic content keeps players engaged and encourages them to return to the game for new experiences.

5. **Scalability:** It allows for the creation of expansive game worlds without significantly increasing development efforts.

In conclusion, combining AI and procedural content generation empowers game developers to create richer, more dynamic, and infinitely replayable gaming experiences. This approach is particularly valuable for open-world games, roguelikes, and games with emergent gameplay elements. As AI technology continues to advance, the possibilities for procedural content generation are limitless, offering exciting opportunities for the future of game development.

Chapter 8: Cutting-Edge Graphics and Rendering

8.1. Advanced Rendering Techniques and Shader Programming

In the world of game development, graphics and rendering are paramount. Achieving stunning visuals and realistic environments is a constant pursuit. This section delves into advanced rendering techniques and shader programming, providing insights into how to push the boundaries of visual fidelity in your CryEngine projects.

Understanding Shaders

Shaders are essential components of modern graphics rendering pipelines. They control various aspects of how objects and materials appear in a scene, including lighting, shadows, reflections, and more. Understanding shaders is crucial for achieving the desired visual effects in your games.

Types of Shaders

1. **Vertex Shader:** Responsible for transforming 3D vertices into 2D screen coordinates.

2. **Pixel Shader (Fragment Shader):** Determines the final color of each pixel rendered on the screen.

3. **Geometry Shader:** Operates on entire primitives (e.g., triangles), allowing for tessellation and geometry manipulation.

4. **Compute Shader:** Used for general-purpose computation on the GPU, enabling tasks like physics simulations and procedural generation.

Shader Programming Languages

Shader code is typically written in specialized programming languages, such as:

- **HLSL (High-Level Shader Language):** Used in DirectX-based systems, including CryEngine.

- **GLSL (OpenGL Shading Language):** Used in OpenGL-based systems.

- **Cg:** A shader programming language developed by NVIDIA.

Advanced Rendering Techniques

1. Physically-Based Rendering (PBR)

PBR is a rendering technique that simulates how light interacts with materials in the real world. It takes into account factors like roughness, metallicity, and specular reflection, resulting in highly realistic materials.

2. Global Illumination (GI)

GI techniques, like radiosity and ray tracing, simulate indirect lighting in a scene. They create soft shadows, color bleeding, and natural ambient lighting, enhancing visual quality.

3. Screen-Space Reflections (SSR)

SSR calculates reflections based on what's visible on the screen, improving the accuracy of reflections while maintaining performance.

4. Ambient Occlusion (AO)

AO adds depth and realism by simulating how ambient light is occluded in corners and crevices.

5. Post-Processing Effects

Effects like motion blur, depth of field, and bloom can be implemented in shaders to enhance the visual appeal of a game.

Code Example: Basic Vertex Shader

```
// Basic vertex shader
struct VertexInput {
    float4 position : POSITION;
    float3 normal : NORMAL;
};

struct VertexOutput {
    float4 position : SV_POSITION;
    float3 normal : NORMAL;
};

VertexOutput main(VertexInput input) {
    VertexOutput output;
    output.position = mul(UNITY_MATRIX_MVP, input.position);
    output.normal = input.normal;
    return output;
}
```

This example showcases a simple vertex shader that transforms 3D vertices into screen space.

Shader Optimization

Optimizing shaders is crucial for maintaining performance. Techniques like loop unrolling, reducing branching, and minimizing texture lookups can significantly impact shader efficiency.

Debugging shaders can be challenging. CryEngine provides tools and plugins to help diagnose shader issues, ensuring that your rendering pipeline runs smoothly.

In the world of advanced graphics and rendering, mastering shader programming and adopting cutting-edge techniques can elevate your game's visual quality to new heights. Whether you're creating realistic environments, stunning visual effects, or immersive virtual worlds, a strong understanding of advanced rendering is a must for CryEngine developers.

8.2. Real-Time Global Illumination and Ray Tracing

Real-time global illumination (RTGI) and ray tracing are groundbreaking techniques that have revolutionized the world of computer graphics. In this section, we explore these technologies and their application in CryEngine to achieve unprecedented levels of realism in your game environments.

Real-Time Global Illumination (RTGI)

RTGI is a rendering technique that simulates the indirect bounce of light within a scene in real time. It significantly enhances the visual quality by providing natural and accurate lighting effects, including:

1. **Global Illumination:** Simulates the interaction of light with surfaces, allowing for realistic color bleeding and soft shadows.

2. **Ambient Occlusion:** Adds depth and realism by simulating the occlusion of ambient light in corners and crevices.

3. **Reflections:** Renders accurate reflections on surfaces, even for dynamic objects and changing environments.

4. **Dynamic Lighting:** Enables dynamic light sources to affect the environment, enhancing realism in interactive scenes.

CryEngine has integrated real-time global illumination techniques to elevate the visual fidelity of your games. This technology is particularly beneficial for creating realistic outdoor environments, architectural visualization, and immersive virtual worlds.

Ray Tracing

Ray tracing is a rendering technique that simulates the behavior of light rays as they interact with objects in a scene. It has gained widespread popularity due to its ability to produce stunning visuals with realistic lighting effects. CryEngine incorporates ray tracing to achieve the following:

1. **Realistic Shadows:** Ray tracing enables the calculation of accurate, soft shadows, improving the overall visual quality.

2. **Ray-Traced Reflections:** Dynamic ray-traced reflections provide highly realistic reflections, even for complex scenes with moving objects.

3. **Global Illumination:** Ray tracing enhances global illumination by accurately simulating light bounces.

4. **Transparency and Refraction:** It accurately handles transparency and refraction effects, such as glass and water.

Code Example: Enabling Ray Tracing in CryEngine

```
// Enabling ray tracing in CryEngine settings
{
    "RayTracing": {
        "Enabled": true,
        "RayTracedReflections": true,
        "RayTracedShadows": true,
        "RayTracedGlobalIllumination": true,
        "RayTracedTransparency": true
    }
}
```

This code snippet demonstrates how to enable ray tracing and its associated features in CryEngine settings. It allows developers to take full advantage of ray tracing capabilities for enhanced visual realism.

Performance Considerations

While real-time global illumination and ray tracing offer unparalleled visual quality, they can be computationally intensive. To maintain good performance, developers should optimize their scenes, use hardware acceleration, and consider the trade-off between visual fidelity and performance.

In conclusion, the integration of real-time global illumination and ray tracing in CryEngine empowers developers to create visually stunning and realistic game environments. These technologies bring cinematic-quality graphics to interactive experiences, making them more immersive and captivating for players. As game development hardware continues to advance, the future holds even more exciting possibilities for pushing the boundaries of realism in video games.

8.3. High-Resolution Texturing and Material Science

High-resolution texturing and material science play a crucial role in modern game development, enabling developers to create immersive and visually stunning virtual worlds. In this section, we delve into the importance of high-resolution textures and the science behind materials in CryEngine.

High-resolution textures are essential for achieving detailed and realistic graphics in games. These textures contain a wealth of visual information, such as surface details, imperfections, and fine details, which contribute to the overall quality of in-game objects and environments. Here are some key aspects of high-resolution textures:

1. **Detail and Realism:** High-resolution textures allow for intricate details, such as fine cracks on a wall, individual grains of sand, or the minute imperfections on a character's skin.

2. **Immersive Environments:** They enhance the sense of immersion by making game worlds feel more tangible and lifelike.

3. **Close-Up Quality:** High-resolution textures ensure that objects still look detailed and convincing when viewed up close.

4. **Visual Consistency:** They help maintain visual consistency across different parts of a game, preventing low-quality textures from standing out.

Materials in CryEngine are the virtual representation of real-world substances, and they play a pivotal role in determining how objects interact with light. CryEngine employs a physically-based rendering (PBR) workflow, which simulates the physical properties of materials to achieve realistic lighting and shading effects. Here are some key concepts in material science within CryEngine:

1. **Albedo (Base Color):** The albedo texture defines the color of a material under direct lighting and serves as a foundation for other material properties.

2. **Normal Maps:** Normal maps add surface detail by simulating small surface imperfections, such as bumps and dents.

3. **Roughness:** The roughness map controls how light is scattered on a material's surface, affecting the perception of glossiness or roughness.

4. **Metallic:** Metallic maps determine whether a material is metallic (reflective) or non-metallic (dielectric).

5. **Ambient Occlusion (AO):** AO maps simulate the areas where light is occluded, enhancing depth and realism.

6. **Emissive Maps:** Emissive maps make certain parts of a material emit light, useful for creating glowing objects or surfaces.

Code Example: Specifying Material Properties in CryEngine

```xml
<Material>
    <Properties>
        <AlbedoMap>textures/brickwall_albedo.dds</AlbedoMap>
        <NormalMap>textures/brickwall_normal.dds</NormalMap>
        <RoughnessMap>textures/brickwall_roughness.dds</RoughnessMap>
        <MetallicMap>textures/brickwall_metallic.dds</MetallicMap>
        <AOMap>textures/brickwall_ao.dds</AOMap>
        <EmissiveMap>textures/brickwall_emissive.dds</EmissiveMap>
    </Properties>
</Material>
```

This XML code snippet demonstrates how to specify material properties in CryEngine. By assigning texture maps for albedo, normal, roughness, metallic, AO, and emissive, developers can fine-tune the appearance of materials to achieve realistic results.

Achieving Visual Excellence

High-resolution texturing and material science are indispensable tools in the game developer's arsenal for achieving visual excellence. They allow developers to create worlds that are not only visually captivating but also emotionally engaging. As technology continues to advance, the potential for even more lifelike graphics in video games continues to grow, promising an exciting future for the medium.

8.4. Visual Effects: From Concept to Implementation

Visual effects (VFX) play a pivotal role in modern game development, enhancing immersion and storytelling by creating stunning and dynamic in-game experiences. In this section, we'll explore the journey of taking VFX from conceptualization to implementation within the CryEngine environment.

Conceptualizing Visual Effects

The process of creating visual effects begins with conceptualization. Game developers and VFX artists work together to define the desired visual style and the role of VFX in conveying the game's narrative and gameplay. Key aspects of conceptualizing visual effects include:

1. **Storyboarding:** Creating a visual storyboard or concept art helps define the look and feel of the effects and their integration into gameplay.

2. **Narrative Alignment:** Ensuring that VFX align with the game's story and lore to create a cohesive experience.

3. **Gameplay Enhancement:** Identifying how VFX can enhance gameplay elements, such as highlighting interactive objects or indicating critical events.

Once the concept is clear, the next step is designing VFX assets. This involves creating textures, particle systems, shaders, and 3D models that bring the visual effects to life. Design considerations include:

1. **Texture Creation:** Designers create custom textures for VFX elements, ensuring they align with the game's art style and theme.

2. **Particle Systems:** Particle systems are used to simulate dynamic effects like fire, smoke, sparks, and explosions.

3. **Shader Development:** Shaders are coded to control the behavior of materials and how they react to light, adding realism to VFX.

4. **Animation:** Animations may be incorporated into VFX to achieve dynamic and fluid effects.

Implementing VFX in CryEngine

CryEngine offers a robust set of tools for implementing VFX seamlessly into your game. Here's an overview of the implementation process:

1. **Integration with CryEngine Sandbox:** VFX assets are imported into the CryEngine Sandbox editor, where designers can visualize and fine-tune their effects in a real-time environment.

2. **Particle Editor:** CryEngine's Particle Editor allows designers to create and control complex particle systems, defining the behavior of particles over time.

3. **Shader Integration:** Shaders are integrated into materials using CryEngine's shader editor, enabling artists to achieve specific visual effects.

4. **Animation Setup:** If VFX involve animations, they can be set up and triggered through CryEngine's animation tools.

Optimization and Performance

Optimizing VFX for performance is crucial to ensure smooth gameplay. CryEngine provides various tools and practices for optimization, including:

1. **Level of Detail (LOD):** Creating multiple LODs for VFX assets to reduce complexity at a distance.

2. **Bounding Boxes:** Implementing bounding boxes for particle systems to reduce their impact on performance when they are not visible.

3. **Texture Compression:** Using texture compression techniques to reduce memory usage.

4. **Particle Culling:** CryEngine's automatic particle culling system helps manage the rendering of particles based on camera proximity.

Iterative Refinement

The process of creating VFX is often iterative. Designers and artists continually refine and adjust effects based on feedback, testing, and how they fit into the overall gameplay experience. This iterative approach ensures that VFX align with the game's vision and enhance player engagement.

In conclusion, visual effects are a powerful tool for elevating game experiences, and CryEngine provides a robust framework for conceptualizing, designing, and implementing stunning VFX. Game developers and artists can harness the full potential of VFX to create immersive and memorable gaming worlds.

8.5. Balancing Visual Fidelity and Performance

Achieving a delicate balance between visual fidelity and performance is a constant challenge in game development. While players expect high-quality visuals, they also demand smooth and responsive gameplay experiences. In this section, we'll delve into strategies and considerations for optimizing visual fidelity without sacrificing performance within the CryEngine ecosystem.

Understanding the Trade-Off

Visual fidelity refers to the quality and realism of graphics in a game. This includes high-resolution textures, detailed character models, realistic lighting, and advanced visual effects. Achieving high visual fidelity often requires substantial computing power and memory bandwidth.

On the other hand, performance relates to the ability of a game to run smoothly on various hardware configurations. This involves maintaining a stable frame rate (usually 30 FPS or higher), minimizing input lag, and ensuring consistent gameplay experiences for players.

The trade-off between visual fidelity and performance arises from the fact that the more complex and detailed the visuals, the more computational resources they consume. Game developers must strike a balance between these two aspects to cater to a broad audience.

CryEngine Optimization Tools

CryEngine provides developers with a range of optimization tools and techniques to help manage visual fidelity and performance effectively:

1. **Level of Detail (LOD):** CryEngine allows developers to create multiple LODs for assets. LODs are simplified versions of models or textures used at different

distances from the camera. This reduces the strain on hardware when objects are farther away.

2. **Texture Streaming:** CryEngine employs a texture streaming system that dynamically loads and unloads textures based on the player's proximity to objects. This helps conserve memory and ensures that only necessary textures are in use.

3. **Lighting Optimization:** CryEngine's lighting system includes features like global illumination and ray tracing, which can be resource-intensive. Developers can adjust settings and use baked lighting techniques to optimize performance.

4. **Geometry Optimization:** CryEngine's optimization tools offer features like automatic polygon reduction and culling to manage the complexity of 3D models, especially in large open-world environments.

Scalability Settings

One effective strategy for balancing visual fidelity and performance is to implement scalability settings. Scalability settings allow players to customize the graphics quality based on their hardware capabilities. CryEngine supports scalability settings that affect various aspects of visuals, such as texture quality, shadow quality, and post-processing effects.

By providing players with scalability options, developers can cater to a broader player base while still offering high-quality visuals to those with powerful gaming rigs.

Profiling and Testing

Profiling tools in CryEngine enable developers to identify performance bottlenecks and areas where visual fidelity can be adjusted for optimization. Regular testing on various hardware configurations is crucial to ensure that the game runs smoothly for all players.

Player Feedback

Developers should actively gather player feedback regarding performance issues and visual quality. This feedback can inform ongoing optimization efforts and help prioritize areas that require improvement.

Conclusion

Balancing visual fidelity and performance is an ongoing process in game development, and it's especially critical for delivering a satisfying player experience. CryEngine provides the tools and flexibility needed to find the right equilibrium between stunning graphics and smooth gameplay, ensuring that your game reaches its full potential on a wide range of gaming platforms.

9.1. Advanced Networking Concepts for Seamless Multiplayer

In this section, we'll explore advanced networking concepts and strategies for creating seamless multiplayer experiences in CryEngine. Multiplayer games are inherently more complex than single-player ones due to the need to synchronize game states across multiple clients and the server. CryEngine provides robust networking features, but mastering them is essential for developing a successful multiplayer game.

Client-Server Architecture

Most multiplayer games, especially those with competitive or cooperative gameplay, utilize a client-server architecture. In this setup, one player acts as the host (server), while others connect as clients. The server is responsible for maintaining the authoritative game state, validating player actions, and broadcasting updates to all clients. Clients send their input to the server, which processes it and sends back the game state.

CryEngine's network system handles client-server communication seamlessly, but developers must consider various aspects:

1. *Server Authority: The server's authority ensures a fair and cheat-free gameplay experience. It's essential to validate client actions on the server to prevent cheating or hacking.*

2. *Bandwidth Optimization: Multiplayer games must minimize the amount of data transferred between clients and the server. CryEngine offers tools for bandwidth optimization, such as reliable and unreliable messages, to prioritize crucial updates.*

3. *Latency Compensation: Dealing with network latency is crucial for responsive gameplay. CryEngine incorporates techniques like client-side prediction and server reconciliation to hide the effects of latency.*

Replication and Networking

CryEngine uses replication to manage the synchronization of game objects and entities across the network. Objects that need to be networked are marked for replication. Developers can define which properties of these objects are relevant for replication and optimize data transfer.

1. *Remote Function Calls (RMI): CryEngine allows developers to call functions on remote objects across the network using Remote Function Calls (RMI). This is useful for triggering events or actions on remote clients.*

2. *Replica Entities: CryEngine supports replica entities, which are synchronized across the network. Developers can specify how replica entities interact with the network and other entities, allowing for precise control over networking behavior.*

Network Security

Security is paramount in multiplayer games to prevent cheating and ensure fair gameplay. CryEngine provides tools for implementing network security measures, including:

*1. **Encryption:** CryEngine supports data encryption to protect sensitive information transmitted between clients and the server.*

*2. **Anti-Cheat Measures:** Implementing anti-cheat measures is essential to maintain a level playing field. CryEngine supports server-side validation and anti-cheat detection mechanisms.*

Scalability and Performance

Scaling multiplayer games to support a large number of players requires careful consideration of server performance and scalability. CryEngine supports server clustering and load balancing, allowing developers to distribute game server instances across multiple machines to handle high player counts.

Testing and Optimization

Thorough testing and optimization are crucial for multiplayer games. Load testing, stress testing, and profiling tools help identify and address performance bottlenecks. CryEngine's built-in profiling tools assist in monitoring network performance and identifying issues.

Conclusion

Creating seamless multiplayer experiences in CryEngine involves mastering advanced networking concepts, maintaining server authority, optimizing bandwidth usage, and implementing security measures. With a strong understanding of CryEngine's networking capabilities, developers can craft engaging multiplayer games that offer a smooth and enjoyable experience for players worldwide.

9.2. Creating Scalable Multiplayer Architectures

In this section, we'll delve into the concept of creating scalable multiplayer architectures for online games using CryEngine. Scalability is essential for accommodating a growing player base and ensuring a smooth gaming experience. CryEngine provides several tools and techniques to design scalable multiplayer systems.

Understanding Scalability

Scalability in multiplayer games refers to the ability to handle an increasing number of players and game instances without sacrificing performance or causing issues like lag or server crashes. There are two primary aspects of scalability:

1. *Vertical Scalability: This involves improving the performance of a single server machine by increasing its resources, such as CPU, RAM, or GPU power. While this can be effective to a certain extent, it has limitations and may not be sufficient for massively multiplayer games.*

2. *Horizontal Scalability: Horizontal scalability focuses on distributing the load across multiple server machines. This approach is more suitable for handling large player bases and ensuring redundancy and fault tolerance.*

Server Clustering

CryEngine supports server clustering, which is a technique for achieving horizontal scalability. Server clustering involves setting up multiple game server instances and distributing players among them. Each server instance is responsible for a specific portion of the game world or a certain number of players. This approach offers several benefits:

1. *Load Balancing: Server clustering distributes player load evenly, preventing overcrowding on a single server. Load balancing ensures that each server maintains optimal performance.*

2. *Fault Tolerance: If one server fails, players can seamlessly transition to other available servers, minimizing disruptions to the gameplay experience.*

3. *Scalability: As the player base grows, additional server instances can be added to the cluster to accommodate more players.*

Server Instances and Zones

CryEngine allows developers to divide the game world into distinct server instances and zones. Each server instance can host a specific region or level of the game. Within each server instance, zones further partition the game world. For example, a large open-world game might have multiple server instances, each containing different zones or areas.

Developers can define rules for player movement between server instances and zones. This approach allows for seamless transitions as players explore different parts of the game world. For instance, when a player crosses a zone boundary, their character's data is transferred to the new server instance, maintaining continuity.

Dynamic Server Allocation

In scenarios where the player population is highly dynamic, CryEngine supports dynamic server allocation. This means that new server instances are created or existing ones are repurposed based on demand. When a server reaches its player capacity, a new server instance is spun up to accommodate additional players. Conversely, if player numbers decrease, unused server instances can be shut down to optimize resource usage.

Synchronization and Data Management

Maintaining consistent game state across multiple server instances is crucial for a seamless multiplayer experience. CryEngine handles synchronization and data management using a combination of replication, network communication, and server-to-server coordination.

Developers can define how data is synchronized between server instances and zones, ensuring that player actions and world updates are reflected accurately to all connected clients.

Creating scalable multiplayer architectures in CryEngine involves understanding both vertical and horizontal scalability concepts. Server clustering, dynamic server allocation, and effective synchronization mechanisms are key components of designing multiplayer systems that can accommodate large and dynamic player bases. With careful planning and implementation, developers can build online games that scale gracefully and provide an enjoyable experience to players of all levels.

9.3. Security and Cheat Prevention Techniques

In this section, we will explore the critical aspects of security and cheat prevention techniques when developing multiplayer games with CryEngine. Ensuring a fair and secure gaming environment is essential to maintain the integrity of your online multiplayer experience.

The Importance of Security

Security in multiplayer games involves protecting the game and its players from various forms of cheating, hacking, and unauthorized access. A breach in security can lead to a negative player experience, loss of player trust, and potential revenue loss. Here are some key security considerations:

1. *Data Integrity: Ensuring that the game's data remains accurate and tamper-free is crucial. This includes preventing unauthorized modifications to player statistics, scores, and in-game assets.*

2. *Fair Play: Cheating can give players an unfair advantage, undermining the competitive balance of the game. This can lead to frustration and dissatisfaction among players.*

3. *Privacy: Protecting player data and personal information is a legal and ethical responsibility. Data breaches can result in legal consequences and damage to your game's reputation.*

Common Cheat Prevention Techniques

To address security concerns, CryEngine provides tools and techniques for cheat prevention:

1. *Server-Side Validation:* *Implement server-side validation for critical game events and actions. This ensures that actions taken by players are legitimate and not manipulated. For example, validate player movements, actions, and interactions on the server to prevent speed hacks or teleportation cheats.*

2. *Encryption:* *Use encryption techniques to secure network communication between clients and servers. This prevents eavesdropping and data tampering. CryEngine supports secure communication protocols for this purpose.*

3. *Anti-Cheat Software:* *Integrate third-party anti-cheat solutions into your multiplayer game. These solutions can detect and prevent various cheating methods, such as aimbots, wallhacks, and scripting cheats.*

4. *Account and Data Security:* *Implement strong user authentication and authorization mechanisms to protect player accounts. Use secure storage and transmission of sensitive data, such as passwords and payment information.*

5. *Regular Updates:* *Keep your game and anti-cheat systems up to date. Cheaters often exploit vulnerabilities in outdated game versions or anti-cheat software.*

6. *Reporting and Monitoring:* *Provide players with a way to report suspected cheaters. Implement monitoring systems to detect unusual player behavior or statistical anomalies that may indicate cheating.*

7. *Punishment System:* *Define and implement a punishment system for cheaters. Penalties may include temporary or permanent bans from the game. Ensure transparency and fairness in the enforcement of penalties.*

Ethical Considerations

While implementing cheat prevention measures, it's essential to strike a balance between security and player experience. Avoid false positives that may incorrectly flag legitimate players as cheaters. Transparency in your cheat detection and punishment systems is crucial to maintain player trust.

Additionally, consider the ethical implications of cheat prevention. Ensure that your security measures respect player privacy and do not collect excessive or unnecessary data.

Conclusion

Security and cheat prevention are ongoing concerns in the world of multiplayer game development. By implementing a combination of server-side validation, encryption, anti-cheat software, and strong user account security, you can create a fair and secure gaming environment that enhances the player experience and maintains the integrity of your multiplayer game. Always stay vigilant, keep your systems up to date, and adapt to emerging cheating techniques to stay one step ahead of potential threats.

9.4. Synchronizing Complex Multiplayer Elements

In this section, we will delve into the intricacies of synchronizing complex multiplayer elements in your CryEngine game. Multiplayer games often involve a variety of dynamic and interactive elements that need to be shared and synchronized among all players in the game session. This synchronization ensures that every player sees a consistent game world and can interact with other players' actions.

Understanding Multiplayer Synchronization

Synchronization in multiplayer games involves updating the game state across all connected clients and the server. Here are some key aspects to consider:

1. *Player Position and Actions: In a multiplayer game, each player's position, movements, and actions must be synchronized with other players. This ensures that all players see the same events happening simultaneously.*

2. *Game World State: The state of the game world, including object positions, physics simulations, and environmental changes, needs to be synchronized among all players. This prevents discrepancies and maintains a consistent game experience.*

3. *Non-Deterministic Events: Some game events may not be entirely deterministic, making synchronization challenging. For example, physics simulations, particle systems, and random events can lead to differences in player experiences.*

4. *Network Latency: Network latency and delays can affect synchronization. Compensation techniques, such as client-side prediction and lag compensation, help mitigate the impact of latency.*

Techniques for Synchronization

CryEngine provides tools and techniques to facilitate synchronization in multiplayer games:

1. **Replication:** *CryEngine's replication system allows you to define which game objects and properties should be replicated to other clients. This allows you to control what information is shared and synchronized across the network.*

2. **Remote Procedure Calls (RPCs):** *Use RPCs to invoke functions on remote clients or the server. RPCs enable you to trigger specific events and actions across all connected players.*

3. **State Synchronization:** *Implement state synchronization for critical game objects and variables. This ensures that all clients maintain a consistent view of the game's state. Use CryEngine's built-in replication features for this purpose.*

4. **Prediction and Lag Compensation:** *To address network latency, employ prediction techniques on the client side. Predictive movement and action handling help maintain smooth gameplay despite network delays.*

5. **Server Authority:** *When resolving conflicting actions or events, prioritize the server's authority. The server's decisions should override those made by individual clients to prevent cheating or discrepancies.*

6. **Delta Compression:** *Optimize data transmission by using delta compression techniques. Transmit only the differences between the current and previous states, reducing bandwidth usage.*

7. **Interpolation:** *Smooth out position and movement updates using interpolation. This improves the visual experience by reducing jitter caused by discrete updates.*

Testing and Debugging

Synchronizing complex multiplayer elements can be challenging, and issues may arise during development. To ensure synchronization works correctly, conduct extensive testing, especially in scenarios with high player counts, varying network conditions, and non-deterministic events.

CryEngine provides debugging tools and console commands to help diagnose synchronization issues. Use these tools to monitor network traffic, inspect replicated data, and identify potential synchronization problems.

Conclusion

Effective synchronization of complex multiplayer elements is essential for creating a seamless and enjoyable multiplayer gaming experience. CryEngine offers a range of features and techniques to facilitate synchronization, from replication and RPCs to prediction and lag compensation. When designing your multiplayer game, prioritize synchronization to ensure that all players have a consistent and fair gaming experience, regardless of their location or network conditions. Regular testing and debugging are crucial to identify and address synchronization issues during development.

9.5. Designing for Massively Multiplayer Online Games (MMOs)

In this section, we will explore the unique challenges and considerations involved in designing and developing games for the massively multiplayer online (MMO) genre using CryEngine. MMOs are known for hosting large numbers of players in a shared virtual world, often with persistent gameplay and complex social interactions. Creating a successful MMO requires careful planning, technical expertise, and a deep understanding of player engagement.

Understanding MMO Game Design

*1. **Scale and Persistence:*** *MMOs operate on a massive scale, accommodating thousands or even millions of concurrent players. The game world must be persistent, meaning it continues to exist and evolve even when players log off. This requires robust server infrastructure and database management.*

*2. **Player Interaction:*** *MMOs thrive on player interaction, including cooperation, competition, and socialization. Designing systems that facilitate meaningful player interactions, such as trading, grouping, and guilds, is crucial.*

*3. **Content Expansion:*** *MMOs often release new content over time to keep players engaged. This includes new quests, areas, items, and storylines. Planning for long-term content updates is essential for the game's sustainability.*

*4. **Economy and Balancing:*** *MMOs typically feature player-driven economies where in-game items and currency hold value. Balancing the economy to prevent inflation and ensuring fair trade is a continuous effort.*

Technical Challenges

*1. **Server Scaling:*** *Supporting a large player base necessitates scalable server architecture. MMOs must handle high concurrency, distribute load efficiently, and maintain server stability.*

*2. **Latency and Lag:*** *Minimizing network latency is crucial for responsive gameplay. Techniques like server clustering, content delivery networks (CDNs), and server location optimization can help reduce lag.*

*3. **Data Management:*** *MMOs generate vast amounts of player data. Efficiently storing, retrieving, and managing player and game world data is essential for smooth operation.*

*4. **Security and Cheating:*** *MMOs are susceptible to cheating and hacking attempts. Robust anti-cheat measures and vigilant monitoring are required to maintain a fair gaming environment.*

Player Retention and Engagement

*1. **Progression Systems:*** *MMOs often employ progression systems, such as character levels, skill trees, and gear upgrades, to keep players engaged. These systems provide long-term goals and a sense of achievement.*

*2. **Social Features:*** *Encouraging social interaction is vital. Features like chat, friend lists, guilds, and in-game events foster a sense of community.*

*3. **Endgame Content:*** *Providing challenging endgame content, such as raids, dungeons, or player versus player (PvP) battles, keeps experienced players invested.*

Monetization Strategies

1. *Subscription Models: Some MMOs adopt subscription models, where players pay a monthly fee for access. This model provides a stable revenue stream for ongoing development.*

2. *Free-to-Play (F2P): Many MMOs are free to play, with revenue generated through microtransactions, in-game purchases, and premium content.*

3. *Cosmetic Items: Selling cosmetic items like skins, costumes, and pets is a popular monetization strategy that doesn't affect gameplay balance.*

Player Feedback and Community

1. *Community Engagement: Actively engage with your player community through forums, social media, and in-game events. Listening to player feedback and addressing concerns builds trust and loyalty.*

2. *Regular Updates: Provide regular content updates, bug fixes, and quality-of-life improvements to show players that the game is continuously evolving.*

Conclusion

Designing and developing an MMO using CryEngine is a complex and challenging endeavor, but it can be immensely rewarding. Success in the MMO genre requires a deep understanding of both game design principles and technical infrastructure. By addressing the unique challenges of MMOs, fostering player engagement, and implementing effective monetization strategies, you can create a thriving virtual world that captures the imagination of players and keeps them coming back for more.

Chapter 10: User Experience and Interface Design

10.1. Advanced UI/UX Design Principles in Game Development

In this section, we will delve into the intricate world of User Interface (UI) and User Experience (UX) design in the context of game development. The user interface is the bridge between players and the virtual world, and crafting a seamless and engaging experience is crucial for player immersion and enjoyment.

Principles of UI/UX Design

1. **Player-Centered Design:** *Always prioritize the player's needs and preferences. Conduct user research to understand your target audience and design interfaces that cater to their expectations.*

2. **Consistency:** *Maintain a consistent visual style and layout throughout the game. Consistency in button placement, color schemes, and fonts enhances usability.*

3. **Clarity and Simplicity:** *Keep UI elements clear and straightforward. Avoid clutter and excessive information. Ensure that essential information is easy to find and understand.*

4. **Feedback and Responsiveness:** *Provide immediate feedback to player actions. Visual and audio cues, such as button highlights or sound effects, confirm interactions, creating a responsive feel.*

Advanced UI Techniques

1. **Dynamic UI:** *Design UI elements that adapt to the game's context. For example, a minimap can change based on the player's location, and health bars can scale according to the character's health.*

2. **Contextual Tooltips:** *Use tooltips to provide additional information when players hover over UI elements. Tooltips are especially useful for explaining complex game mechanics or item descriptions.*

3. **Customization:** *Allow players to customize the UI to suit their preferences. This includes resizing, repositioning, or even changing the color scheme of UI elements.*

Accessibility and Inclusivity

1. **Accessibility Options:** *Implement accessibility features, such as adjustable font sizes, colorblind modes, and keyboard shortcuts, to ensure that all players can enjoy the game.*

2. **Testing with Diverse Audiences:** *Conduct usability testing with individuals of varying abilities and backgrounds to identify and address potential accessibility issues.*

Analytics and User Feedback

1. **Data-Driven Design:** *Utilize player analytics to make informed decisions about UI/UX improvements. Track player behavior, monitor UI usage, and gather feedback to drive iterative design.*

2. **User Feedback Loops:** *Establish channels for players to provide feedback, such as forums, in-game surveys, or dedicated feedback systems. Actively listen to player input and prioritize improvements based on their suggestions.*

User Onboarding

1. *Tutorial and Onboarding:* Design a user-friendly tutorial that gradually introduces players to game mechanics and UI elements. Avoid overwhelming new players with complex information.

2. *Progressive Disclosure:* Present information progressively as players advance in the game. Start with basic UI elements and gradually introduce more advanced features.

Conclusion

Advanced UI/UX design is a critical aspect of game development, impacting player engagement and overall enjoyment. By following user-centered design principles, embracing advanced techniques, ensuring accessibility, and leveraging player feedback, you can create an intuitive and immersive user interface that enhances the gaming experience and keeps players coming back for more.

10.2. Creating Customizable and Dynamic Interfaces

In this section, we will explore the concept of customizable and dynamic interfaces in game development. Customization plays a significant role in enhancing the player's experience, allowing them to tailor the game's UI to their preferences and needs. Additionally, dynamic interfaces adapt to in-game situations, providing real-time information and improving usability.

The Importance of Customization

Customizable interfaces empower players to personalize their gaming experience. This not only increases player satisfaction but also accommodates diverse player preferences and accessibility requirements. Here are key considerations for creating customizable interfaces:

1. *Layout and Positioning:* *Allow players to rearrange UI elements, change their size, and reposition them on the screen. Providing flexibility in UI layout enables players to optimize their view.*

2. *Color Schemes:* *Offer a variety of color themes or allow players to choose their own color combinations. Consider implementing colorblind-friendly options to ensure inclusivity.*

3. *HUD Elements:* *Enable players to toggle on or off specific Heads-Up Display (HUD) elements, such as minimaps, health bars, or quest trackers. This declutters the screen and reduces information overload.*

4. *Key Binding:* *Provide options for players to customize key bindings and control schemes. This is especially important for PC games that may have complex control setups.*

Implementing Customization

To implement customizable interfaces, consider the following approaches:

1. *Settings Menu:* *Create a dedicated settings menu where players can adjust UI-related preferences. Provide clear explanations for each option to help players make informed choices.*

2. *Drag-and-Drop UI Editor:* *Develop an intuitive UI editor that allows players to drag and drop UI elements to their desired positions on the screen. Ensure that changes take effect immediately.*

3. *Color Palette Selection:* *Include a color palette selection feature that lets players choose from predefined color schemes or create their own. Ensure that chosen colors maintain readability.*

4. *Save and Load Profiles:* *Allow players to save their UI customization settings as profiles. This feature enables them to switch between different setups easily.*

Dynamic Interfaces

Dynamic interfaces adapt to in-game situations, providing real-time information to players. Here are some dynamic UI elements commonly used in games:

1. *Dynamic Maps:* *Implement maps that update in real-time to reflect the player's current location, discovered areas, and points of interest.*

2. *Objective Trackers:* *Display current quests, objectives, and progress dynamically on the screen. Highlight the most relevant information based on the player's goals.*

3. *Status Indicators:* *Show real-time status indicators, such as health, mana, or ammunition, prominently on the screen. Use visual cues like color changes or animations to convey critical information.*

Responsive Design

Responsive design is essential for both customizable and dynamic interfaces. Ensure that UI elements adapt gracefully to different screen sizes and aspect ratios, especially when developing games for various platforms.

Consider conducting usability testing with players of different skill levels to gather feedback on the effectiveness of your customizable and dynamic UI. Iteratively refine the UI based on this feedback to create a polished and player-centric interface.

In summary, customizable and dynamic interfaces enhance the player experience by allowing personalization and providing real-time information. Implementing these features can set your game apart and create a more inclusive and engaging gaming environment.

10.3. Implementing Intuitive Controls and Feedback Systems

In this section, we will delve into the importance of intuitive controls and feedback systems in game development. Intuitive controls are essential for providing a smooth and enjoyable gaming experience, while feedback systems help players understand the consequences of their actions and the state of the game world. Together, they contribute to player engagement and satisfaction.

Designing Intuitive Controls

Intuitive controls are user-friendly and easy to learn, allowing players to interact with the game world effortlessly. Here are some best practices for designing intuitive controls:

1. *Consistency: Maintain consistency in control schemes across similar actions or mechanics. For example, use the same button or key for jumping in different situations.*

2. *Mapping: Map controls logically to in-game actions. For instance, use the trigger button for shooting in first-person shooters, aligning with players' real-world expectations.*

3. *Progressive Complexity: Introduce controls gradually, especially in tutorials or early game stages. Start with simple actions and gradually introduce more complex ones as players become familiar with the basics.*

4. *Accessibility: Consider players with varying levels of gaming experience. Offer customizable control schemes, including options for different input devices and accessibility features such as one-handed controls.*

5. *User Testing: Conduct usability testing with players to gather feedback on control schemes. Adjust controls based on player input to ensure they feel natural and responsive.*

Feedback Systems

Feedback systems provide players with information about their actions and the state of the game world. Effective feedback enhances player immersion and understanding. Here are key aspects to consider when implementing feedback systems:

1. *Visual Feedback: Use visual cues such as animations, particle effects, and on-screen prompts to indicate the outcome of actions. For example, displaying a health bar decreasing when a character takes damage provides clear visual feedback.*

2. *Auditory Feedback: Incorporate sound effects and audio cues to complement visual feedback. Audio feedback can indicate success, failure, or important events in the game.*

3. *Haptic Feedback: On platforms that support it, use haptic feedback, such as controller vibrations, to immerse players further. Vibration patterns can convey different sensations, from footsteps to explosions.*

4. *Progress Indicators: Show players their progress towards objectives, goals, or achievements. Progress bars, score counters, and mission updates are common examples.*

5. *Error Messages: When players make mistakes or encounter issues, provide clear and informative error messages. Avoid generic messages that do not help players understand the problem.*

Testing and Iteration

Testing is crucial for ensuring that controls and feedback systems work as intended. Conduct playtesting with a diverse group of players to identify any issues or areas for improvement. Consider the following:

1. Usability Testing: Observe how players interact with the controls and assess whether they find them intuitive. Make adjustments based on their feedback.

2. Feedback Elicitation: Ask players for feedback on the clarity and helpfulness of in-game feedback systems. Determine whether they understand the consequences of their actions and the game's state.

3. Accessibility Testing: Ensure that control options and feedback are accessible to players with disabilities. Test with assistive technologies and gather feedback from players with disabilities to make necessary adjustments.

4. Balancing: Balance the level of feedback to avoid overwhelming players with excessive information. Adjust feedback based on player feedback and playtesting results.

Incorporating intuitive controls and effective feedback systems into your game design can significantly enhance the player experience. Players who can easily understand and interact with your game are more likely to be engaged and satisfied, leading to a more successful and enjoyable gaming experience.

10.4. Accessibility and Inclusivity in UI Design

Accessibility and inclusivity in UI (User Interface) design are vital considerations for game developers. Ensuring that your game can be enjoyed by players of all abilities and backgrounds not only broadens your potential audience but also promotes a more inclusive and ethical approach to game development. In this section, we'll explore the principles and practices of creating accessible and inclusive UIs.

Understanding Accessibility

Accessibility refers to designing products and environments that can be used by individuals with a wide range of abilities and disabilities. In the context of games, accessibility means making your game playable and enjoyable by everyone, regardless of their physical or cognitive abilities. Here are some key aspects of accessibility in UI design:

1. **Keyboard and Controller Support:** *Ensure that all game actions and menu navigation can be performed using both keyboard and controller inputs. This is crucial for players who may have limited mobility or prefer specific input methods.*

2. **Text Size and Readability:** *Use legible fonts and provide options to adjust text size. Some players may have visual impairments or prefer larger text for readability.*

3. **Color Contrast:** *Maintain good color contrast in your UI elements to make them easily distinguishable. This benefits players with color blindness or low vision.*

4. **Audio Accommodations:** *Include subtitles or closed captions for dialogue and important audio cues. This assists players with hearing impairments or those who prefer to play games without sound.*

5. **Customizable Controls:** *Allow players to remap controls to suit their preferences and needs. This empowers players to adapt the game to their individual requirements.*

Inclusive UI Design

Inclusivity goes beyond accessibility and aims to create UIs that welcome and represent diverse player communities. Here are some strategies for inclusive UI design:

1. **Representation:** *Ensure that your game's UI and artwork are culturally sensitive and respectful. Avoid stereotypes and aim for diverse representation in characters and imagery.*

2. **Language Support:** *Provide localization and translation options to make your game accessible to players from different linguistic backgrounds.*

3. **Gender-Inclusive Design:** *Avoid gender-specific language or imagery unless it is essential to the game's narrative. Make character customization options flexible to accommodate diverse gender identities.*

4. **Sensitivity to Sensitive Topics:** *Be mindful of potentially triggering or sensitive content and provide content warnings or options to skip such content.*

5. **Community Engagement:** *Actively engage with your player community and seek feedback on the inclusivity of your game. Listen to their suggestions and concerns and make improvements accordingly.*

User Testing and Feedback

To ensure the accessibility and inclusivity of your game's UI, it's essential to conduct user testing with a diverse group of players. Include individuals with disabilities and people from various backgrounds in your testing process. Collect feedback on the usability, accessibility, and inclusivity of your UI, and be prepared to iterate and make improvements based on this feedback.

By prioritizing accessibility and inclusivity in your UI design, you not only create a more welcoming gaming experience but also contribute to a positive and ethical gaming industry.

Players of all backgrounds and abilities will appreciate your efforts, and your game will become more enjoyable and accessible to a wider audience.

10.5. Analytics and User Feedback: Refining the User Experience

Analytics and user feedback play a crucial role in game development, allowing developers to refine the user experience, identify areas for improvement, and make data-driven decisions. In this section, we'll delve into the importance of analytics and user feedback and how they can be leveraged to enhance your game.

The Value of Analytics

Analytics involve the collection, measurement, and analysis of data related to player behavior, in-game events, and user interactions. This data-driven approach provides several benefits:

1. *Player Understanding:* *Analytics help you gain insights into how players engage with your game. You can track player progression, playtime, and preferred gameplay styles.*

2. *Identifying Pain Points:* *By analyzing data, you can pinpoint areas where players struggle or encounter frustration. This information guides improvements in level design, tutorials, or gameplay mechanics.*

3. *Feature Prioritization:* *Data helps prioritize which features or content updates are most important based on player preferences and needs.*

4. *Balancing and Fine-Tuning:* *Analytics assist in balancing game mechanics, weapons, and character abilities. You can adjust parameters based on real player data rather than assumptions.*

5. *Monetization Strategies:* *For free-to-play or monetized games, analytics inform decisions about in-game purchases, advertisements, and pricing models.*

Collecting User Feedback

In addition to analytics, user feedback is an invaluable resource for developers. Feedback can come from various sources, including in-game surveys, community forums, social media, and player reviews. Here's how to effectively collect user feedback:

1. **In-Game Surveys:** *Implement surveys within the game to gather player opinions and preferences. Ask about their satisfaction, suggestions for improvement, and favorite aspects of the game.*

2. **Community Engagement:** *Actively participate in and monitor community forums, social media platforms, and Discord channels related to your game. Listen to player discussions and respond to their questions and concerns.*

3. **Review Analysis:** *Pay attention to player reviews on platforms like Steam, Google Play, and the App Store. Identify recurring themes in both positive and negative reviews.*

4. **Player Support:** *Provide players with a way to report bugs and technical issues within the game. Respond promptly to support requests and keep players informed about bug fixes and updates.*

5. **Beta Testing:** *Conduct beta testing phases to gather feedback from a select group of players before the official release. Beta testers can identify issues and provide valuable input.*

Continuous Iteration

Once you've collected analytics and user feedback, the next step is to use this information for continuous iteration. Here's how this process typically works:

1. **Data Analysis:** *Analyze the collected data to identify patterns, anomalies, and areas for improvement. Look for trends in player behavior and preferences.*

2. **Feedback Prioritization:** *Prioritize feedback and issues based on severity and impact on the player experience. Some issues may require immediate attention, while others can be addressed in future updates.*

3. **Development and Testing:** *Implement changes and improvements based on the analyzed data and feedback. Test these changes thoroughly to ensure they don't introduce new issues.*

4. **Deployment:** *Release updates, patches, or hotfixes to the game, addressing the identified issues and incorporating player-suggested improvements.*

5. **Communication:** *Keep players informed about the changes you've made based on their feedback. Transparency and communication are essential for maintaining player trust.*

Ethical Considerations

While analytics and user feedback are powerful tools, it's crucial to handle player data and feedback ethically and responsibly. Respect player privacy, anonymize data when possible, and obtain informed consent for data collection. Additionally, be open to criticism and receptive to feedback, even when it's negative, and prioritize the well-being and satisfaction of your player community.

In conclusion, analytics and user feedback are indispensable for refining the user experience, enhancing gameplay, and making data-driven decisions in game development.

By actively collecting and analyzing this information and using it for continuous iteration, you can create a more enjoyable and engaging gaming experience while fostering a positive relationship with your player community.

Chapter 11: Mobile and Cross-Platform Development

Section 11.1: Advanced Strategies for Mobile Game Development

Mobile game development has witnessed a remarkable surge in recent years, thanks to the widespread adoption of smartphones and tablets. As game developers, it's essential to explore advanced strategies to create compelling and successful mobile games. In this section, we'll delve into various aspects of mobile game development, including optimization, user interface design, performance considerations, and monetization strategies.

Understanding the Mobile Landscape

Before embarking on mobile game development, it's crucial to understand the mobile gaming landscape. This involves researching market trends, analyzing successful mobile games, and identifying the target audience. Mobile gamers have diverse preferences, so catering to specific niches or genres can be a viable strategy. Whether you're developing for iOS, Android, or both platforms, knowing the audience and market is fundamental.

Choosing the Right Game Engine

Selecting the appropriate game engine for mobile development is pivotal. Engines like Unity, Unreal Engine, and CryEngine have gained popularity for their cross-platform capabilities. They offer tools and features tailored for mobile development, allowing you to streamline the development process and optimize performance.

Optimizing for Mobile Performance

Mobile devices come in various hardware configurations, making performance optimization a critical aspect of mobile game development. Optimizing graphics, reducing memory usage, and employing efficient rendering techniques are essential. Additionally, implementing adaptive graphics settings can ensure a smooth gaming experience across a range of devices.

Crafting Engaging Gameplay for Mobile

Mobile games often differ from their console or PC counterparts in terms of gameplay mechanics. Touchscreen controls, accelerometer inputs, and gestures provide unique opportunities and challenges. Designing intuitive and responsive controls is crucial for player engagement. Mobile games should also consider shorter play sessions, as players may prefer to pick up and play during brief intervals.

User Interface and User Experience (UI/UX)

Creating an intuitive and visually appealing user interface (UI) is vital for mobile games. Players should navigate menus, interact with in-game elements, and access information seamlessly. Effective UI/UX design enhances player retention and overall satisfaction. Consider incorporating user feedback and conducting usability tests to refine the UI/UX.

Monetization Strategies

Monetizing mobile games can be achieved through various strategies, including in-app purchases, advertisements, and premium pricing models. Choosing the right monetization approach depends on your game's genre, target audience, and goals. Implementing a combination of strategies can provide a diversified revenue stream.

Cross-Platform Challenges

Cross-platform development enables your game to reach a broader audience. However, it also poses challenges related to compatibility, performance, and user experience. Ensuring a consistent experience across different platforms is essential. Cross-platform development tools and frameworks can simplify the process while maintaining quality.

Adapting to Emerging Technologies

Mobile game development doesn't stand still. Emerging technologies like augmented reality (AR) and cloud gaming are transforming the landscape. Being open to adopting new technologies and adapting your games to these trends can set you apart from the competition.

Conclusion

Mobile game development offers exciting opportunities for developers to create innovative and engaging experiences. By understanding the mobile gaming ecosystem, optimizing performance, designing intuitive UI/UX, and adopting effective monetization strategies, you can navigate the complexities of mobile game development and bring your vision to a global audience.

Section 11.2: Cross-Platform Play: Challenges and Solutions

Cross-platform play, where players on different gaming platforms can play together in the same multiplayer environment, has become increasingly popular and expected by gamers. However, implementing cross-platform play comes with its own set of challenges and complexities. In this section, we'll explore these challenges and discuss potential solutions for creating a seamless cross-platform gaming experience.

The Appeal of Cross-Platform Play

Cross-platform play offers several benefits. It expands the player base, reduces matchmaking times, and fosters a more vibrant and engaged community. Players can enjoy their favorite games with friends, regardless of the devices they use. It also extends the lifespan of games by maintaining an active player community long after the initial release.

Compatibility and Fairness

One of the primary challenges of cross-platform play is ensuring compatibility and fairness among players using different input methods and hardware capabilities. For example, a player using a keyboard and mouse may have an advantage over someone using a touchscreen or a game controller. To address this challenge, game developers can implement input-based matchmaking, grouping players with similar input methods. Additionally, developers can design game mechanics that level the playing field, reducing the impact of input disparities.

Technical Hurdles

Cross-platform play requires robust networking solutions to connect players on various platforms. Games must handle differences in network protocols, latency, and synchronization. Using standardized networking libraries and frameworks can simplify this process. Developers should also implement server-authoritative gameplay to prevent cheating and ensure a consistent experience.

User Account Integration

To enable cross-platform play, games often require user accounts or profiles. Developers must provide a smooth account integration process, allowing players to link their accounts across different platforms easily. This involves handling account authentication, data synchronization, and maintaining consistent player progression.

Cross-Platform Voice and Text Chat

Communication is crucial in multiplayer games. Implementing cross-platform voice and text chat systems that work seamlessly across different platforms can be a complex task. Leveraging third-party services or APIs for chat functionality can help streamline this process while ensuring clear and secure communication.

Updates and Patch Management

Managing updates and patches for cross-platform games can be challenging. Different platforms may have varying submission and approval processes, which can lead to delays in delivering updates. To mitigate this, developers should plan ahead, communicate with platform providers, and strive to release updates simultaneously across all platforms.

Security and Cheat Prevention

Maintaining the integrity of cross-platform play requires robust security measures. Cheat prevention mechanisms should be in place to detect and deter cheaters across all platforms. Implementing a report system that allows players to report suspicious behavior can also aid in maintaining fair play.

Player Communities and Support

Cross-platform games often have diverse player communities with varying expectations and needs. Developers should actively engage with these communities, listen to feedback, and provide support for issues specific to each platform. Community managers can help bridge communication between players and developers.

Legal and Licensing Considerations

Developers must be aware of legal and licensing considerations when implementing cross-platform play. Licensing agreements with platform providers and adherence to platform-specific terms of service are essential. Legal experts or consultation with platform providers can help navigate these complexities.

Conclusion

Cross-platform play presents exciting opportunities for game developers to create inclusive and thriving gaming communities. While it comes with its share of challenges, addressing compatibility, technical hurdles, account integration, communication systems, updates, security, and community support can lead to a successful cross-platform gaming experience that satisfies players and promotes long-term engagement. As technology continues to evolve, cross-platform play is likely to become an even more prominent aspect of the gaming landscape, making it a valuable skill for game developers to master.

Section 11.3: Performance Optimization Across Different Devices

In the realm of mobile and cross-platform game development, optimizing performance across a wide range of devices is a critical aspect of ensuring a smooth and enjoyable player experience. Unlike developing for a single, homogeneous platform, creating games for multiple devices with varying hardware capabilities presents unique challenges. This section delves into the importance of performance optimization and provides strategies for achieving optimal gameplay across different devices.

The Device Diversity Challenge

Mobile and cross-platform games can run on a plethora of devices, each with its own CPU, GPU, memory, and screen specifications. From high-end smartphones and tablets to budget devices, the hardware capabilities vary significantly. As a developer, your goal is to ensure your game performs well across this spectrum.

Profiling and Benchmarking

Profiling and benchmarking are essential tools for identifying performance bottlenecks and measuring the efficiency of your game on different devices. Profiling tools allow you to analyze the CPU and GPU usage, memory consumption, and frame rate. Benchmarking involves running your game on various devices to gather performance data.

Efficient Asset Management

Proper asset management is vital for performance optimization. Create multiple versions of assets at different resolutions and quality settings, and load the appropriate version based on the device's capabilities. Implement asset streaming and resource pooling to minimize memory usage.

Graphics Optimization

Graphics optimization is crucial for maintaining a smooth frame rate. Use level-of-detail (LOD) models to reduce the polygon count of distant objects. Employ occlusion culling to avoid rendering objects that are not visible to the camera. Consider using a dynamic resolution scaling system that adjusts the rendering resolution based on the device's performance.

```csharp
// Example dynamic resolution scaling in Unity (C#)
void Update()
{
    float performanceFactor = CalculatePerformanceFactor(); // Adjust based on performance metrics
    int targetWidth = Screen.width;
    int targetHeight = Screen.height;

    // Adjust the target resolution based on performance
    targetWidth = Mathf.RoundToInt(targetWidth * performanceFactor);
    targetHeight = Mathf.RoundToInt(targetHeight * performanceFactor);

    // Set the target resolution
    Screen.SetResolution(targetWidth, targetHeight, true);
}
```

Multithreading and Asynchronous Loading

Leverage multithreading and asynchronous loading to distribute CPU-intensive tasks and reduce loading times. For example, background loading of assets and level data can prevent frame rate drops during gameplay. Ensure proper synchronization to avoid race conditions and ensure thread safety.

```cpp
// Example multithreading with C++ and std::thread
#include <thread>

void LoadAssetsInBackground()
{
    // Load assets asynchronously here
}

int main()
{
    // Start asset loading thread
    std::thread assetThread(LoadAssetsInBackground);
```

```
    // Continue with the main game logic

    // Wait for the asset loading thread to complete
    assetThread.join();

    return 0;
}
```

UI and User Interface Optimization

Optimizing the user interface (UI) is essential for mobile and cross-platform games. Use efficient UI libraries and frameworks that are optimized for performance. Minimize the use of complex UI animations and effects, especially on devices with limited processing power.

Device-Specific Settings

Allow players to adjust graphics and performance settings within the game to cater to their device's capabilities. Provide options to reduce graphical fidelity, adjust rendering quality, or disable resource-intensive features like real-time shadows or post-processing effects.

Regular Testing and QA

Testing your game on a variety of devices is an ongoing process. Conduct regular quality assurance (QA) testing to identify performance issues and compatibility problems on different hardware configurations. Encourage player feedback and bug reports to address performance-related issues promptly.

Conclusion

Performance optimization across different devices is a continuous effort that requires careful planning, profiling, and testing. By implementing strategies like efficient asset management, graphics optimization, multithreading, UI optimization, device-specific settings, and regular testing, you can create a mobile and cross-platform game that delivers a consistent and enjoyable experience for players, regardless of their chosen device.

Section 11.4: Leveraging Cloud Technologies for Cross-Platform Play

In the ever-evolving landscape of game development, leveraging cloud technologies has become a powerful tool for achieving cross-platform play. Cloud computing offers scalable solutions for various aspects of game development, including multiplayer infrastructure, data storage, and real-time communication. This section explores the benefits of incorporating cloud technologies into your mobile and cross-platform games and provides insights into how to effectively utilize these resources.

Cloud technologies encompass a wide range of services provided by cloud providers like Amazon Web Services (AWS), Microsoft Azure, Google Cloud Platform (GCP), and others. These services include:

1. **Multiplayer Servers**: Cloud providers offer managed multiplayer server solutions that simplify the development of cross-platform multiplayer games. These services handle the server infrastructure, player matchmaking, and real-time communication, allowing you to focus on game logic.

2. **Data Storage**: Cloud-based databases and storage solutions provide secure and scalable options for storing game data, player profiles, and user-generated content. This data can be accessed from any device with an internet connection, enabling seamless cross-platform experiences.

3. **Content Delivery**: Content delivery networks (CDNs) ensure fast and reliable delivery of game assets, reducing loading times and latency. This is particularly important for mobile and cross-platform games where network conditions vary.

4. **Analytics and Telemetry**: Cloud platforms offer analytics and telemetry services that allow you to collect and analyze player data, monitor game performance, and make data-driven decisions for game improvement and monetization.

Achieving Cross-Platform Play

To implement cross-platform play using cloud technologies, consider the following strategies:

1. Multiplayer Servers as a Service

Utilize managed multiplayer server solutions offered by cloud providers. These services automatically handle server scaling, matchmaking, and real-time communication. By using these services, you ensure that players on different platforms can seamlessly connect and play together.

2. Cross-Platform Authentication

Implement cross-platform authentication and user account management using cloud-based identity providers. This allows players to use a single account across multiple devices and platforms, preserving their progress and purchases.

3. Synchronized Data Storage

Leverage cloud databases to synchronize player progress, game state, and user-generated content across platforms. This ensures that players can access their data from any device, enhancing the cross-platform experience.

```
// Example of synchronizing player data using cloud-based database (JavaScript)
```

```
const database = cloudProvider.createDatabaseInstance();
const playerId = getCurrentPlayerId();

// Save player progress to the cloud
database.savePlayerProgress(playerId, gameProgress);

// Load player progress on a different device
const loadedProgress = database.loadPlayerProgress(playerId);
```

4. Real-Time Communication

Implement real-time communication channels using cloud messaging services. This enables players on different platforms to interact with each other in real-time, enhancing the social aspects of your game.

```python
# Example of real-time chat using cloud messaging service (Python)
import cloudMessaging

def sendChatMessage(message):
    cloudMessaging.sendMessage(message)

def receiveChatMessage():
    return cloudMessaging.receiveMessage()
```

5. Cloud-Based Game Logic

Consider offloading computationally intensive game logic to cloud functions or serverless computing platforms. This allows you to maintain consistent gameplay experiences across devices, regardless of their processing power.

Security and Privacy Considerations

When utilizing cloud technologies, prioritize security and player privacy. Implement robust security measures, encryption, and access controls to protect player data. Ensure compliance with data protection regulations, and communicate your data usage and privacy policies clearly to players.

Conclusion

Leveraging cloud technologies for cross-platform play opens up new opportunities for game developers to reach a wider audience and provide seamless gaming experiences. By incorporating managed multiplayer servers, synchronized data storage, cross-platform authentication, real-time communication, and cloud-based game logic, you can create mobile and cross-platform games that break down the barriers between devices and platforms, fostering a connected and engaged player community.

Section 11.5: Developing for Emerging Platforms and Technologies

The world of game development is in a constant state of evolution, driven by emerging platforms and technologies. Staying ahead of the curve and adapting to these innovations can be a key factor in the success of your game development career. In this section, we'll explore the exciting possibilities and challenges presented by emerging platforms and technologies in the gaming industry.

Exploring Emerging Platforms

1. *Virtual Reality (VR) and Augmented Reality (AR)*: VR and AR technologies have gained significant traction in recent years. Developing games for VR and AR offers immersive experiences and new gameplay possibilities. Ensure your game design takes full advantage of these platforms by integrating spatial computing, gesture recognition, and 3D audio.

2. *Cloud Gaming*: Cloud gaming services like Google Stadia, NVIDIA GeForce Now, and Xbox Cloud Gaming (formerly Project xCloud) are changing the way games are delivered and played. Consider adapting your game to run on these platforms, allowing players to stream and play on various devices with minimal hardware requirements.

```
// Example of cloud gaming integration (C#)
using CloudGamingSDK;

void Start()
{
    CloudGaming.Initialize();
    CloudGaming.LoadGame("YourGameTitle");
}
```

3. *Mobile Devices*: As smartphones and tablets continue to advance in hardware capabilities, mobile gaming is becoming increasingly sophisticated. Explore ways to optimize your games for high-end mobile devices, making use of touch controls, gyroscopes, and AR capabilities.

4. *Wearable Technologies*: Smartwatches, smart glasses, and other wearables are emerging as potential gaming platforms. Develop games that utilize the unique features of these devices, such as health tracking, haptic feedback, and voice commands.

Challenges of Emerging Technologies

While emerging platforms offer exciting opportunities, they also come with challenges:

1. *Hardware Fragmentation*: With various VR headsets, cloud gaming services, and mobile devices on the market, ensuring compatibility and performance across different hardware configurations can be a daunting task.

2. *User Experience*: Emerging technologies often require new user interfaces and interaction paradigms. Striking the right balance between innovation and usability is crucial for a successful user experience.

3. *Market Adoption*: The adoption rate of emerging platforms can vary, and not all players may have access to them. Consider the size and demographics of your target audience when deciding to develop for a specific platform.

Staying Agile and Adaptable

To thrive in the ever-changing landscape of emerging technologies, adopt an agile development approach. Be willing to experiment, iterate, and pivot as needed. Engage with developer communities and stay informed about the latest trends and advancements in the industry.

```python
# Example of agile development mindset (Python)
def adapt_to_change():
    while True:
        if emerging_technology():
            be_ready_to_pivot()
        else:
            continue_with_current_plan()
```

Conclusion

Developing for emerging platforms and technologies is an exciting journey that can lead to groundbreaking games and innovative experiences. Embrace the challenges, stay adaptable, and remain at the forefront of technological advancements to create games that captivate players on the platforms of tomorrow. The gaming industry will continue to evolve, and as a developer, you have the opportunity to shape its future.

Chapter 12: Virtual and Augmented Reality

Section 12.1: Advanced VR and AR Development in CryEngine

Virtual Reality (VR) and Augmented Reality (AR) have revolutionized the way we experience digital content. VR immerses users in entirely virtual worlds, while AR enhances the real world with digital elements. These technologies have found significant applications in gaming, training, education, and various industries. In this section, we'll delve into advanced VR and AR development using CryEngine, exploring the techniques and best practices for creating immersive experiences.

Understanding VR and AR

1. *Virtual Reality (VR)*: *VR transports users into a fully immersive digital environment, typically through a headset that tracks head movement and sometimes hand controllers for interaction. It provides a sense of presence and immersion that traditional gaming cannot match.*

2. *Augmented Reality (AR)*: *AR overlays digital information onto the real world, often using smartphones or AR glasses. It blends the virtual and physical, opening up opportunities for interactive experiences in various settings.*

Developing VR and AR Games with CryEngine

3. *CryEngine VR Support*: *CryEngine offers VR support, allowing you to create VR experiences for a range of VR headsets, including Oculus Rift, HTC Vive, and Windows Mixed Reality. To enable VR mode in CryEngine, you can use the following code snippet:*

```
// Enable VR mode in CryEngine (C++)
void EnableVRMode()
{
    gEnv->pSystem->GetIConsole()->ExecuteString("vr_enable 1");
}
```

4. *Optimizing for VR*: VR applications demand high performance and low latency to prevent motion sickness. Optimize your VR game by reducing unnecessary rendering, implementing dynamic level-of-detail (LOD) systems, and maintaining a consistent frame rate.

Design Principles for Immersive Experiences

5. *User Interface (UI) in VR and AR*: Designing UI elements for VR and AR requires careful consideration. Ensure that UI elements are placed within the user's field of view and are easy to interact with using motion controllers or gestures.

6. *Spatial Audio*: Utilize 3D spatial audio to enhance the sense of presence in VR. Sound should be accurately positioned in 3D space to match visual cues, creating a more convincing environment.

7. *Interactivity*: In VR, user interaction is vital for immersion. Implement hand tracking or motion controllers to enable natural interactions with virtual objects and environments.

Challenges and Future Trends

8. *Hardware Limitations*: VR and AR development must account for the limitations of current hardware, such as screen resolution, field of view, and tracking accuracy. As hardware improves, developers can create more realistic experiences.

9. *Social VR*: The future of VR includes social interactions in virtual spaces. Consider integrating multiplayer features and social experiences to tap into this growing trend.

10. *Mixed Reality*: Combining VR and AR elements in mixed reality experiences offers exciting possibilities. As AR glasses become more prevalent, developers can explore blending digital and real-world elements seamlessly.

Conclusion

Advanced VR and AR development in CryEngine opens up a world of possibilities for creating immersive and interactive experiences. As these technologies continue to evolve, game developers have the opportunity to push the boundaries of storytelling, gameplay, and user engagement. Embrace the challenges, stay updated on hardware advancements, and design experiences that transport players to new realities. Virtual and augmented reality are at the forefront of the gaming industry's future, and your creativity can help shape it.

Section 12.2: Creating Immersive and Interactive VR/AR Experiences

Creating immersive and interactive Virtual Reality (VR) and Augmented Reality (AR) experiences is a thrilling endeavor that demands a deep understanding of both technology and user experience. In this section, we'll explore the key aspects of crafting such experiences using CryEngine.

Defining Immersion in VR/AR

1. *Presence*: Immersion in VR/AR is often described in terms of "presence," where users feel like they're truly inside the digital world. Achieving presence requires high-quality graphics, low latency, and accurate tracking.

2. *Spatial Audio*: Audio plays a crucial role in immersion. Spatial audio, where sounds are positioned in 3D space, enhances the sense of being in a virtual environment. CryEngine supports spatial audio technologies to achieve this effect.

Storytelling and Gameplay

3. *Narrative Engagement*: VR/AR can provide unique narrative opportunities. Engage users by crafting compelling stories that take full advantage of the immersive capabilities. Consider branching narratives and interactive storytelling elements.

4. *Interactivity*: Interactive elements are at the core of VR/AR experiences. Design intuitive controls and interactions that allow users to manipulate objects, solve puzzles, or participate actively in the story.

Designing for Comfort

5. *Motion Sickness Mitigation*: Some users may experience motion sickness in VR. Implement comfort features like teleportation, snap-turning, or field-of-view adjustments to minimize discomfort.

6. *User Interface (UI)*: UI design in VR/AR differs significantly from traditional screen-based UIs. Ensure that UI elements are readable, easily accessible, and designed with user comfort in mind.

Technical Considerations

7. *Optimization*: VR/AR experiences demand high performance. Optimize your project by reducing rendering overhead, implementing efficient asset loading, and using techniques like occlusion culling.

8. *Cross-Platform Compatibility*: Consider developing for multiple VR/AR platforms. CryEngine supports various VR headsets, so ensure your project is compatible with the intended devices.

Prototyping and Testing

9. *Rapid Prototyping*: Iteration is crucial in VR/AR development. Use rapid prototyping to test ideas quickly and gather user feedback. Tools like CryEngine's Sandbox Editor facilitate this process.

10. *User Testing*: Involve real users in the testing phase. Collect feedback on comfort, gameplay, and overall experience to make informed design decisions.

Future Trends

11. *Hand and Gesture Tracking*: As VR/AR hardware evolves, hand and gesture tracking technologies will become more prevalent. Consider incorporating these technologies to enhance user interactions.

12. *Haptic Feedback*: Advanced haptic feedback systems can provide tactile sensations, further enhancing immersion. Explore integrating haptic devices for a more sensory-rich experience.

Conclusion

Creating immersive and interactive VR/AR experiences in CryEngine is an exciting journey that combines technical expertise, creative storytelling, and user-centered design. By embracing the unique capabilities of VR and AR, you can transport users to captivating digital worlds where they can engage, explore, and experience stories like never before. Stay informed about emerging technologies and user preferences to continue pushing the boundaries of what's possible in this rapidly evolving field. VR/AR development in CryEngine offers limitless potential for innovative and memorable experiences.

Section 12.3: Designing for VR/AR Hardware and Limitations

Designing for Virtual Reality (VR) and Augmented Reality (AR) hardware requires a deep understanding of the capabilities and limitations of the target devices. In this section, we'll explore the key considerations when creating VR/AR experiences in CryEngine that are optimized for specific hardware platforms.

Hardware Diversity

*1. **VR/AR Headsets**: VR and AR experiences are primarily driven by headsets such as Oculus Rift, HTC Vive, HoloLens, or mobile devices like the Oculus Quest. Each headset has distinct features, input methods, and performance levels, necessitating platform-specific development.*

*2. **Input Devices**: VR/AR platforms offer various input methods, including motion controllers, hand tracking, and traditional gamepads. Design your interactions to align with the hardware available on the target platform.*

Performance Optimization

*3. **Frame Rate**: Maintaining a consistent and high frame rate is crucial for VR/AR comfort and immersion. CryEngine provides performance optimization tools to ensure your project runs smoothly on different hardware.*

*4. **Graphics Settings**: Adjust graphical settings, such as texture quality, shadow resolution, and anti-aliasing, to strike a balance between visual fidelity and performance, depending on the target hardware's capabilities.*

Field of View (FoV)

*5. **FoV Considerations**: VR headsets offer varying degrees of field of view. Ensure that your content is designed to work within the FoV limitations of the target hardware to prevent objects from being cut off or distorted.*

*6. **UI Placement**: When designing user interfaces (UI) in VR/AR, take into account the FoV and avoid placing critical UI elements outside the user's view.*

Tracking and Movement

*7. **Tracking Precision**: Different VR/AR systems offer varying levels of tracking precision. Plan your interactions and gameplay mechanics accordingly to account for tracking limitations.*

*8. **Motion Sickness**: Implement comfort features such as teleportation, smooth locomotion options, or vignettes to reduce motion sickness, especially for users prone to discomfort.*

Display and Resolution

*9. **Screen Resolution**: VR/AR headsets have different screen resolutions. Optimize your content for the target resolution to ensure clarity and readability.*

*10. **Text Legibility**: Pay special attention to text legibility in VR/AR. Use larger fonts and high-contrast text to ensure readability.*

Audio Design

*11. **Spatial Audio**: Leverage CryEngine's spatial audio capabilities to enhance immersion. Ensure that audio sources are positioned accurately in 3D space to match the user's perspective.*

12. *Audio Performance*: Consider the audio performance of the target hardware. Some VR/AR devices may have limited audio processing capabilities, so optimize audio assets accordingly.

User Comfort

13. *Comfort Settings*: Provide users with options to customize comfort settings, such as adjusting movement speed or enabling/disabling comfort features. This allows users to tailor their experience to their comfort level.

14. *Testing and Feedback*: Regularly test your VR/AR experiences on the target hardware and gather user feedback to identify and address comfort issues.

Platform-Specific Features

15. *Platform SDKs*: Utilize platform-specific software development kits (SDKs) to access unique features of VR/AR hardware. These SDKs may offer access to hand tracking, gesture recognition, or device-specific capabilities.

16. *App Store Guidelines*: If you plan to release your VR/AR experience on app stores or platforms like Oculus Store or SteamVR, adhere to their guidelines and requirements to ensure compatibility and approval.

Future-Proofing

17. *Future Hardware*: Stay informed about upcoming VR/AR hardware releases and updates. Design your experiences with flexibility to adapt to new technologies and features.

18. *Cross-Platform Development*: Consider developing your VR/AR project to be cross-platform compatible, allowing it to reach a broader audience and future-proofing it against hardware changes.

Designing for VR/AR hardware in CryEngine requires a balance between technical optimization, user comfort, and adherence to platform-specific guidelines. By considering the unique characteristics of each target hardware platform and continuously testing and iterating on your VR/AR experiences, you can create immersive and engaging content that takes full advantage of the capabilities of these evolving technologies.

Section 12.4: Spatial Computing and Mixed Reality Integration

Spatial computing and mixed reality (MR) represent the convergence of the physical and digital worlds, offering exciting opportunities for immersive experiences. In this section, we'll explore how to leverage spatial computing and seamlessly integrate mixed reality into your CryEngine projects.

Spatial computing is the ability of computers to interact with and manipulate the physical world. It involves technologies like augmented reality (AR), virtual reality (VR), and mixed reality (MR). In MR, digital content is overlaid onto the real-world environment, creating a blended experience.

Key Concepts:

1. **Spatial Mapping**: MR devices use sensors to scan and map the physical environment. Understanding the spatial layout is crucial for placing digital content accurately.

2. **Anchor Points**: Anchor points are fixed locations in the physical world that digital objects can attach to. They help maintain consistency between the real and virtual elements.

Integrating Mixed Reality

CryEngine can be used to create compelling MR experiences by combining 3D assets, real-world mapping data, and interaction design. Here are essential considerations for MR integration:

1. Hardware Compatibility: Determine which MR headsets or devices your project will support. Ensure your chosen hardware provides spatial mapping and tracking capabilities.

2. Spatial Awareness: Leverage spatial mapping data to recognize and understand the real-world environment. This allows digital objects to interact realistically with physical surfaces and objects.

3. Realistic Anchoring: Use anchor points to attach digital content to specific locations in the real world. This ensures that virtual objects stay in place relative to the physical environment.

4. Interaction Design: Design intuitive interactions that blend seamlessly with the real world. Hand gestures, voice commands, and physical controllers can enhance user engagement.

5. Spatial Sound: Implement spatial audio to enhance the sense of presence. Sounds should originate from their corresponding virtual objects' locations in the physical space.

6. Visual Occlusion: Address occlusion challenges by ensuring that virtual objects realistically hide behind physical objects in the user's view.

7. User Calibration: Allow users to calibrate their MR experience for comfort and accuracy. This may involve adjusting the spatial mapping quality or controller sensitivity.

8. Performance Optimization: MR experiences demand high performance. Optimize your project to maintain a consistent frame rate and responsiveness.

9. User Safety: Ensure that users can navigate the MR environment safely. Implement features like collision detection to prevent physical collisions.

10. Testing and Feedback: Regularly test your MR experience with the target hardware and gather user feedback. Iterate on design and functionality to improve the user's mixed reality experience.

Development Tools and SDKs

To develop MR experiences in CryEngine, you may need to use specific SDKs and tools provided by MR platform providers. For example, Microsoft's HoloLens offers the Mixed Reality Toolkit (MRTK) for Unity, which can be adapted for use with CryEngine.

Applications of Mixed Reality

Mixed reality has applications beyond gaming, including:

- **Training and Simulation**: MR can simulate real-world scenarios for training purposes, such as medical training or industrial equipment operation.

- **Remote Collaboration**: MR allows users in different locations to collaborate within a shared mixed reality space.

- **Architectural Visualization**: Architects can use MR to visualize building designs in real-world contexts, allowing for better decision-making.

- **Education**: MR enhances educational experiences by providing interactive, immersive learning environments.

- **Product Design and Prototyping**: MR enables designers to visualize and interact with product prototypes in the real world.

Mixed reality is a rapidly evolving field that opens up exciting creative possibilities. By understanding the principles of spatial computing and following best practices for MR integration, you can create engaging and immersive mixed reality experiences using CryEngine.

Section 12.5: Future Trends in VR/AR Gaming

Virtual Reality (VR) and Augmented Reality (AR) have made significant strides in the gaming industry, revolutionizing how players interact with digital worlds. As technology continues to advance, new trends are emerging in VR/AR gaming. In this section, we'll explore some of these exciting developments.

1. Wireless VR/AR Experiences

One of the key trends in VR/AR gaming is the move towards wireless experiences. Tethered VR headsets have limitations in terms of mobility and comfort. Emerging technologies are now enabling fully wireless VR and AR devices. This trend allows players to move freely in the physical space without being constrained by cables, enhancing immersion.

2. Improved Haptic Feedback

Haptic feedback plays a crucial role in VR/AR gaming by providing tactile sensations. Future trends involve more advanced haptic feedback solutions that offer a wider range of sensations, such as pressure, temperature, and texture. This will create more realistic and engaging experiences.

3. Eye-Tracking and Foveated Rendering

Eye-tracking technology is becoming increasingly prevalent in VR/AR headsets. By tracking the user's gaze, these systems can optimize rendering by focusing on the area the user is looking at (foveated rendering). This results in improved performance and reduced hardware requirements.

4. Enhanced Social and Multiplayer Experiences

VR/AR gaming is moving towards more social and multiplayer interactions. Virtual social spaces and collaborative gaming experiences are gaining popularity. Developers are creating environments where players can interact with friends and other users, fostering a sense of community within the virtual world.

5. Realistic Avatars and Personalization

Advancements in scanning and modeling technology allow for highly realistic avatars in VR/AR environments. Users can create digital representations of themselves with incredible fidelity. This trend enhances personalization and immersion.

6. AI-Driven NPCs and Environments

AI-driven characters and environments are evolving to be more dynamic and responsive in VR/AR games. NPCs exhibit more human-like behavior, making interactions more engaging. Procedural generation and machine learning are being used to create immersive worlds that adapt to player actions.

7. Cross-Platform Compatibility

Developers are focusing on making VR/AR games compatible across different platforms and devices. This trend allows players with various hardware setups to enjoy the same experiences, promoting inclusivity and expanding the player base.

8. Health and Comfort

As VR/AR gaming becomes more mainstream, there is an increasing emphasis on user health and comfort. Features like adaptive comfort settings and regular breaks are being integrated to reduce motion sickness and discomfort during extended play sessions.

9. Integration with Real-World Data

AR gaming is exploring opportunities to integrate real-world data into gameplay. Location-based AR games, such as Pokémon GO, use geolocation and mapping data to create interactive experiences in the player's physical surroundings. This trend is likely to continue evolving.

10. Accessibility and Inclusivity

Accessibility features are becoming standard in VR/AR games. Developers are incorporating options for players with disabilities, such as customizable controls, subtitles, and audio descriptions, ensuring that everyone can enjoy these immersive experiences.

Conclusion

The future of VR/AR gaming holds exciting possibilities, driven by technological advancements and evolving player expectations. As these trends continue to shape the industry, game developers will have the opportunity to create even more immersive, engaging, and inclusive virtual and augmented reality experiences for players worldwide. Keeping an eye on these developments will be essential for staying at the forefront of this dynamic field.

Chapter 13: Procedural Generation and Dynamic Content

Procedural generation is a powerful technique in game development that involves creating content algorithmically rather than manually. It allows developers to generate vast, diverse, and dynamic game worlds, levels, and assets, often with minimal storage requirements. In this chapter, we'll delve into the fascinating world of procedural generation and explore how it can be harnessed to enhance gameplay and extend a game's lifespan.

Section 13.1: Implementing Procedural Generation Techniques

Procedural generation encompasses a wide range of techniques and applications. Here, we'll focus on how to implement procedural generation effectively in your games.

Understanding the Basics

At its core, procedural generation involves using algorithms to create content. This content can include terrain, level layouts, textures, game objects, and even narrative elements. To get started, you'll need a solid understanding of programming and data structures.

Randomness and Seeds

A fundamental aspect of procedural generation is randomness. Random numbers and seeds are used to ensure that each generated instance is unique. Seeds allow you to reproduce specific results, which can be useful for debugging and sharing procedurally generated content.

```python
import random

# Setting a seed for reproducibility
random.seed(42)

# Generating a random number
value = random.randint(1, 100)
```

Noise Functions

Noise functions, like Perlin noise and Simplex noise, are essential tools in procedural generation. They create smoothly changing values that are often used to generate terrain heightmaps, textures, and more. Libraries like LibNoise provide easy-to-use implementations of noise functions.

Procedurally Generated Terrain

Generating realistic terrain is a common application of procedural generation. You can create heightmaps and use noise functions to displace vertices, creating mountains, valleys, and hills. Combine this with texture generation to produce detailed and varied landscapes.

```
# Pseudocode for terrain generation
for x in range(width):
    for y in range(height):
        height_value = noise(x, y)   # Use noise function
        set_vertex_height(x, y, height_value)
```

Dungeon and Level Generation

Procedural generation is frequently employed to create dungeons, levels, and mazes. Algorithms like cellular automata and recursive division can be used to generate intricate and randomized layouts for gameplay.

Asset Variation and Diversity

Procedural generation isn't limited to terrain and level layouts. You can also use it to diversify game assets. For example, generating variations of trees, rocks, or buildings with different colors, sizes, and shapes can add visual richness to your game.

Balancing and Testing

While procedural generation offers endless possibilities, it's crucial to balance the generated content to ensure fair gameplay. Testing is essential to identify and address issues such as unfair level layouts or overly difficult challenges.

Dynamic Content Updates

Procedural generation isn't limited to the initial game release. You can use it to introduce dynamic content updates, adding new quests, items, or areas to keep players engaged long after the game's launch.

Conclusion

Procedural generation is a valuable tool for game developers seeking to create expansive, dynamic, and engaging experiences. By mastering the techniques and principles outlined in this section, you'll be equipped to implement procedural generation effectively in your games, providing players with fresh and exciting content each time they play.

Section 13.2: Creating Dynamic Game Worlds and Environments

In this section, we will explore how to leverage procedural generation to create dynamic and ever-changing game worlds and environments. Dynamic worlds add replayability and depth to your game, making each playthrough a unique experience.

The Power of Dynamic Environments

Static game worlds can become predictable after repeated playthroughs, leading to reduced player engagement. Dynamic environments, on the other hand, keep players on their toes, offering fresh challenges and surprises each time they play.

Procedural World Generation

To create dynamic game worlds, you'll need a robust procedural world generation system. This system can generate landscapes, weather patterns, ecosystems, and more. Consider the following aspects:

Terrain Generation

Procedural terrain generation can produce diverse landscapes with mountains, valleys, forests, and rivers. By combining noise functions and fractal algorithms, you can create realistic and visually appealing terrain.

```
# Generate terrain heightmap
def generate_terrain(width, height, seed):
    terrain = []
    for x in range(width):
        column = []
        for y in range(height):
            height_value = noise(x, y, seed)
            column.append(height_value)
        terrain.append(column)
    return terrain
```

Weather and Climate Systems

Dynamic weather systems add immersion to your game. Implement weather patterns, such as rain, snow, and storms, using procedural generation. Combine temperature, humidity, and wind algorithms to create believable climates.

Ecosystems and Biomes

Procedurally generated ecosystems and biomes can dictate the distribution of flora and fauna in your game world. Define rules for plant and animal behavior, ensuring diversity and realism.

Dynamic Events

Incorporate dynamic events like earthquakes, wildfires, and migrations. These events can reshape the game world, creating new challenges and opportunities for players.

Player Interaction and Impact

To make dynamic environments truly engaging, allow players to interact with and influence them. Consider these ideas:

Player Choices

Enable players to make decisions that impact the world. Choices could affect weather patterns, wildlife behavior, or the overall state of the environment.

Resource Management

Introduce resource management mechanics, where players must balance resource consumption and conservation. Over-harvesting or polluting could have lasting effects on the environment.

Environmental Feedback

Provide players with feedback on their actions' environmental impact. Show how their decisions affect the ecosystem, weather, and world events.

Balancing Challenges

Creating dynamic game worlds is exciting, but it's essential to balance the difficulty and ensure fairness. Use playtesting and data analytics to fine-tune the procedural generation algorithms and make adjustments as needed.

Conclusion

Dynamic game worlds and environments breathe life into your game, offering players a constantly evolving experience. By embracing procedural generation techniques, you can create immersive and engaging worlds that captivate players and keep them coming back for more.

Section 13.3: Algorithmic Content Creation and Variation

In this section, we'll delve into algorithmic content creation and variation, which can significantly enhance your game's replayability and content richness. With the right algorithms, you can generate diverse levels, quests, characters, and more, ensuring that no two playthroughs are the same.

Algorithmic Level Design

Algorithmic level design is the art of generating game levels procedurally. By defining rules and parameters, you can create a wide range of levels without the need for manual design. Consider the following techniques:

Maze Generation

Mazes can be generated using algorithms like Prim's or Kruskal's to create complex and challenging levels. These mazes can serve as dungeons, labyrinths, or puzzle areas within your game.

```python
# Generate a maze using Prim's algorithm
def generate_maze(width, height):
    # Initialize grid
    grid = [[1] * width for _ in range(height)]

    # Choose a random starting point
    start_x, start_y = random.randint(0, width - 1), random.randint(0, height - 1)
    grid[start_y][start_x] = 0

    # Create a list of walls to consider
    walls = [(x, y) for x in range(width) for y in range(height) if x % 2 == 1 or y % 2 == 1]

    while walls:
        wall_x, wall_y = random.choice(walls)
        neighbors = [(wall_x + dx, wall_y) for dx in (-2, 2)] + [(wall_x, wall_y + dy) for dy in (-2, 2)]
        random.shuffle(neighbors)

        for neighbor_x, neighbor_y in neighbors:
            if 0 <= neighbor_x < width and 0 <= neighbor_y < height:
                if grid[neighbor_y][neighbor_x] == 0:
                    continue

                opposite_x, opposite_y = wall_x + (neighbor_x - wall_x) // 2, wall_y + (neighbor_y - wall_y) // 2
                if grid[opposite_y][opposite_x] == 0:
                    grid[wall_y][wall_x] = 0
                    grid[neighbor_y][neighbor_x] = 0
                    walls.remove((wall_x, wall_y))
                    break

    return grid
```

Procedural Quest Generation

Generate quests with randomized objectives, characters, and locations. Quests can vary in complexity and difficulty, providing players with unique challenges during each playthrough.

Diverse Enemy Encounters

Use algorithms to spawn different types and combinations of enemies in various locations. Adjust enemy behavior and abilities to keep combat encounters engaging and unpredictable.

Character and NPC Variation

Algorithmic character and NPC generation can add depth to your game world. Here are some approaches:

Character Appearance

Create a wide range of character appearances by mixing and matching attributes like hairstyle, clothing, and accessories. Randomize these attributes to produce diverse NPCs.

Personality Traits

Assign personality traits and behaviors to NPCs using algorithms. This can influence how they interact with the player, other NPCs, and the game world.

Dynamic Storytelling

Algorithmic storytelling involves generating narrative elements, such as branching dialogues, plot twists, and character arcs, based on player choices and game events. This ensures that each playthrough results in a unique narrative experience.

Balancing and Testing

When implementing algorithmic content creation, it's crucial to maintain balance and ensure that generated content is enjoyable. Regular playtesting and fine-tuning of algorithms are essential to achieve this balance.

Conclusion

Algorithmic content creation and variation empower game developers to create rich, dynamic, and endlessly replayable experiences. By embracing procedural generation techniques for levels, quests, characters, and narratives, you can captivate players with a constantly evolving world, keeping them engaged and excited for each new playthrough.

Section 13.4: Balancing Randomness and Design in Procedural Generation

Balancing randomness and design in procedural generation is a critical aspect of game development. While randomness can create diverse and unpredictable gameplay experiences, excessive randomness can lead to frustration or monotony. Striking the right balance between procedural content and carefully crafted design is essential for a successful game.

The Role of Randomness

Randomness is often used in procedural generation to introduce variability into game elements such as level layouts, loot drops, and enemy spawns. It can add excitement and replayability by ensuring that no two playthroughs are exactly the same. However, uncontrolled randomness can result in levels that are too chaotic, quests that make no sense, or difficulty spikes that frustrate players.

Designing Rules and Constraints

To balance randomness, it's crucial to design rules and constraints that guide the procedural generation process. These rules help ensure that the generated content adheres to predefined criteria, maintaining a level of consistency and quality.

Example: Random Dungeon Generation

Consider a procedural dungeon generation system. Instead of allowing random placement of traps and monsters, you can define rules to ensure that:

- The dungeon has a logical layout with a clear path to the goal.
- Monsters are placed strategically to provide a gradual increase in difficulty.
- Traps are located in areas where players have a chance to detect and avoid them.

By implementing these rules, you strike a balance between randomness and design, creating challenging but fair gameplay experiences.

Player-Centric Design

Balancing randomness and design should always be player-centric. You must consider how the generated content will impact the player's experience. Content that is too random or too designed can both lead to player frustration.

Iterative Testing and Feedback

Iterative testing and player feedback are invaluable for finding the right balance. Playtesters can provide insights into whether the procedural generation enhances or detracts from the game's enjoyment. Developers can then adjust algorithms and rules accordingly.

Dynamic Difficulty Adjustment

Procedural generation can also be used for dynamic difficulty adjustment. By analyzing player performance and behavior, the game can adapt its generated content to provide an appropriate level of challenge.

Adaptive Enemy Scaling

For instance, if players consistently find combat encounters too easy, the game can increase the stats and abilities of enemies in subsequent levels. Conversely, if players struggle with difficulty spikes, the game can reduce enemy numbers or provide additional resources.

Conclusion

Balancing randomness and design in procedural generation is an ongoing process that requires careful consideration and testing. When done effectively, it can elevate your game by providing variety, replayability, and a tailored experience for each player. Finding the right balance ensures that procedural content remains engaging and enjoyable throughout the entire game.

Section 13.5: Infinite Gameplay: Extending Game Lifespan through Dynamic Content

One of the challenges in game development is keeping players engaged for an extended period. Dynamic content generation is a powerful tool to achieve this goal. By creating a system that continuously generates new content, you can provide players with an ever-evolving experience that keeps them coming back for more.

The Appeal of Infinite Gameplay

Infinite gameplay refers to the idea that players can continue enjoying a game indefinitely without exhausting its content. This concept has gained popularity in genres such as roguelikes, sandbox games, and online multiplayer experiences. The allure of infinite gameplay lies in its ability to offer:

- **Endless Variety**: With dynamic content generation, each playthrough or session can be different. New levels, quests, challenges, and items can be introduced, ensuring that players always have something fresh to explore.

- **Longevity**: Games with infinite gameplay can remain relevant and enjoyable for years. This longevity can lead to a dedicated player base and ongoing revenue opportunities.

- **Player Progression**: Players can continue to progress, gain achievements, and improve their skills over time. This sense of advancement keeps them engaged and motivated.

Procedural Generation for Infinite Gameplay

Procedural generation is a key technique for implementing infinite gameplay. It enables developers to create vast amounts of content algorithmically, reducing the need for manual design and art creation. Here are some ways procedural generation can be applied:

Randomized Maps and Levels

Infinite gameplay often relies on randomized or procedurally generated maps and levels. This approach ensures that players never encounter the exact same layout twice. For example, in a roguelike game, each dungeon run can offer a unique level layout, enemy placement, and loot distribution.

```python
# Pseudocode for random map generation
def generate_random_map(width, height):
    map = create_empty_map(width, height)
    for _ in range(num_rooms):
        room = generate_random_room()
        if is_room_valid(room, map):
            place_room(room, map)
    return map
```

Dynamic Quests and Challenges

Dynamic quests and challenges can be generated based on player progress, ensuring that there's always a new objective to pursue. For instance, in an open-world RPG, the game can generate side quests, bounties, or exploration challenges as players explore the game world.

```javascript
// Example of dynamically generated quest
function generateRandomQuest(playerLevel) {
    const questTypes = ['Hunt', 'Retrieve', 'Explore'];
    const randomType = questTypes[Math.floor(Math.random() * questTypes.length)];
    const questLevel = playerLevel + Math.floor(Math.random() * 3) - 1;
    return {
        type: randomType,
        level: questLevel,
        description: generateQuestDescription(randomType, questLevel),
        reward: generateQuestReward(questLevel),
    };
}
```

Procedural Items and Loot

Infinite gameplay often includes a wide variety of items, weapons, and equipment. Procedural generation can be used to generate these items with random attributes, creating a diverse loot pool. This keeps players engaged as they search for rare and powerful gear.

```csharp
// C# example of procedurally generated item
public class ProceduralItem {
    public string Name { get; set; }
    public ItemType Type { get; set; }
    public int Rarity { get; set; }
    public int Damage { get; set; }
    public int Defense { get; set; }
    // ... other properties and methods
}
```

Balancing Challenges and Progression

While dynamic content generation is a fantastic tool for infinite gameplay, it's crucial to balance the difficulty and progression curve. Players should face increasingly challenging content as they become more skilled or progress through the game. Balancing ensures that the game remains engaging without becoming too easy or frustratingly difficult.

Community and Player Input

Incorporating player feedback and involving the community can be invaluable for creating dynamic content. Players can suggest new challenges, quests, or content ideas, making them feel part of the game's ongoing development. Community-driven content can extend a game's lifespan and foster a dedicated player base.

Conclusion

Dynamic content generation is a powerful technique for achieving infinite gameplay and extending the lifespan of a game. By utilizing procedural generation, balancing challenges, and involving the community, developers can create games that players enjoy for years, ensuring the game's success and longevity in the competitive gaming industry.

Chapter 14: Game Analytics and Player Data

Section 14.1: Utilizing Analytics for Game Design and Improvement

In the ever-evolving landscape of game development, data-driven decision-making has become increasingly important. Game analytics provide developers with valuable insights into player behavior, allowing for informed design choices and continuous improvement. In this section, we'll explore the significance of analytics in game development and how to harness their power for better games.

The Role of Game Analytics

Game analytics involve the collection, processing, and interpretation of data generated by players during their interactions with a game. This data encompasses a wide range of metrics, including player actions, in-game events, and user demographics. The primary roles of game analytics are as follows:

1. **Understanding Player Behavior**: Analytics help developers gain insights into how players engage with their game. By tracking actions such as player movement, interactions, and progression, developers can understand player preferences and pain points.

2. **Balancing and Tuning**: Game balance is crucial for an enjoyable player experience. Analytics can reveal imbalances, allowing developers to fine-tune gameplay, difficulty, and item distributions to ensure fairness and engagement.

3. **Content Creation and Optimization**: Data on player preferences and content completion rates can guide the creation of new content and updates. Developers can focus on creating content that resonates with players and optimizing underutilized areas.

4. **Monetization Strategies**: For free-to-play games, analytics are essential for optimizing monetization models. By analyzing player spending behavior, developers can design effective in-game purchases and advertisements that enhance revenue without compromising the player experience.

Implementing Game Analytics

To leverage game analytics effectively, developers should follow a structured approach:

1. **Data Collection**: Implement systems to collect relevant data points, such as player actions, events, and performance metrics. Game engines and third-party tools offer solutions for data tracking.

2. **Data Storage**: Store collected data securely and efficiently, either locally or on remote servers. Cloud-based solutions are popular for scalability and ease of access.

3. **Data Processing**: Process and clean the collected data to remove noise and inconsistencies. This step ensures that the analytics are based on accurate information.

4. **Visualization and Interpretation**: Use data visualization tools to create charts, graphs, and reports that make the data understandable. Interpret the results to draw meaningful conclusions.

5. **Iterative Analysis**: Continuously analyze player data to identify trends and patterns. Regular analysis allows for swift adjustments and improvements.

6. **Feedback Loop**: Incorporate the insights gained from analytics into the game's design and development process. Iterate on the game based on player behavior and preferences.

Privacy and Ethical Considerations

While game analytics offer numerous advantages, it's crucial to handle player data responsibly and ethically. Ensure that you comply with data protection laws and regulations, and be transparent with players about data collection practices. Respect player privacy and avoid intrusive data collection methods.

Conclusion

Game analytics are a valuable tool for enhancing game design, optimizing player experiences, and maximizing revenue in the gaming industry. When used ethically and effectively, analytics can be a game changer, helping developers create games that captivate and retain players for the long term. In the next sections, we will delve deeper into specific aspects of game analytics, including player behavior tracking, interpreting analytics, and data-driven design decisions.

Section 14.2: Tracking and Interpreting Player Behavior

Tracking and interpreting player behavior through game analytics is a crucial aspect of game development. Understanding how players interact with your game can guide design decisions, improve user experience, and increase player retention. In this section, we'll delve into the process of tracking and interpreting player behavior using analytics.

Collecting Player Behavior Data

To begin tracking player behavior, you need to collect relevant data points. These data points can include:

1. **Player Actions**: Record every action players take within the game, such as movement, attacks, item usage, and interactions with non-playable characters (NPCs).

2. **Events and Milestones**: Track significant in-game events and milestones, such as level completions, achievements unlocked, or boss battles won.

3. **Progression Metrics**: Monitor player progression through the game, including level advancement, completion percentages, and time spent on different activities.

4. **User Demographics**: Gather information about your player base, including age, location, device type, and other demographics that can help tailor your game to your audience.

5. **Monetization Metrics**: If your game includes in-app purchases or advertisements, track player spending behavior, ad engagement, and conversion rates.

Analyzing Player Behavior

Once you've collected data, the next step is to analyze it to gain actionable insights. Here are some key aspects to consider during the analysis:

1. **Player Paths**: Visualize the paths players take through your game. Identify common routes, bottlenecks, and areas where players tend to drop off. This information can help you improve level design and player progression.

2. **Retention Rates**: Analyze player retention rates to understand how long players continue to engage with your game. Identify points in the game where retention drops significantly and work on improving those sections.

3. **Engagement Metrics**: Look at metrics related to player engagement, such as session lengths, frequency of play, and daily active users. Determine what keeps players coming back for more.

4. **Conversion Funnel**: If your game includes monetization elements, create a conversion funnel to track the player journey from initial download to making in-game purchases. Optimize the funnel to maximize revenue.

5. **A/B Testing**: Implement A/B testing to compare different game features, UI elements, or monetization strategies. Analyze which variations perform better and iterate accordingly.

Iterative Game Design

One of the primary benefits of tracking and interpreting player behavior is the ability to iterate on your game's design. Use the insights gained from analytics to make informed decisions about gameplay mechanics, level design, difficulty balancing, and content updates.

For example, if analytics reveal that most players struggle with a particular boss battle, you can adjust the boss's abilities or provide additional in-game hints to improve the player experience. Similarly, if a specific in-app purchase is not performing well, you can refine the pricing or offer better value to players.

Game analytics should complement player feedback. Encourage players to provide feedback and pay attention to their comments and suggestions. Sometimes, player feedback can reveal issues or opportunities that analytics alone may not uncover.

In conclusion, tracking and interpreting player behavior through game analytics is an essential practice for game developers. It enables data-driven decision-making, helps in optimizing player experiences, and ultimately contributes to the success of your game. By continuously analyzing player behavior and integrating the insights into your game's design and development process, you can create a more engaging and enjoyable gaming experience for your audience.

Section 14.3: Data-Driven Game Design Decisions

Data-driven game design is a practice that leverages analytics and player behavior data to make informed decisions throughout the development process. In this section, we'll explore how data-driven game design can lead to better gameplay experiences and higher player engagement.

The Role of Data in Game Design

Traditional game design often relies on intuition, creativity, and experience. While these aspects are crucial, data can provide an objective and empirical foundation for design decisions. Here's how data plays a role in game design:

1. **Balancing and Tuning**: Data allows designers to fine-tune gameplay elements such as character abilities, weapon stats, enemy behavior, and resource distribution. By analyzing player interactions, designers can adjust these variables to create a balanced and enjoyable experience.

2. **Level Design**: Data-driven level design involves analyzing how players navigate and engage with levels. Heatmaps and player paths can reveal where players get stuck, where they excel, and what areas need improvement.

3. **Content Creation**: Data can guide the creation of in-game content, including quests, missions, and challenges. Designers can identify which types of content are most popular and create more of what players enjoy.

4. **Monetization**: In games with in-app purchases, data helps optimize monetization strategies. By tracking player spending behavior and conversion rates, designers can tailor pricing and offers to maximize revenue without compromising player satisfaction.

To implement data-driven game design, you need a robust data collection and analysis pipeline:

1. **Data Collection**: Collect relevant data points, including player actions, events, progression, and demographic information. Implement analytics tools or services within your game to automatically gather this data.

2. **Data Storage**: Store the collected data securely, ensuring compliance with data privacy regulations. Cloud-based solutions and databases are common choices for data storage.

3. **Data Analysis**: Employ data analysts or data scientists to interpret the collected data. They can create reports, dashboards, and visualizations to uncover insights.

4. **Iterative Design**: Use the insights gained from data analysis to make iterative design decisions. Test changes, gather more data, and refine your design further.

Examples of Data-Driven Design Decisions

Let's look at some examples of how data-driven game design decisions can positively impact a game:

1. Balancing Characters:
- Data shows that one character class has an exceptionally high win rate in multiplayer matches.
- Designers adjust the character's abilities and attributes to level the playing field.
- Subsequent data analysis reveals improved balance and a more competitive environment.

2. Level Difficulty:
- Heatmaps indicate that players consistently struggle with a particular level section.
- Designers modify the level layout and enemy placements based on this data.
- Players' success rates increase, leading to higher player satisfaction.

3. In-Game Store Optimization:
- Data reveals that only a small percentage of players make in-app purchases.
- Designers experiment with pricing, discounts, and limited-time offers.
- Conversion rates improve, resulting in increased revenue without alienating non-paying players.

Challenges and Ethical Considerations

While data-driven game design offers numerous benefits, it comes with challenges and ethical considerations:

1. **Data Privacy**: Ensure that you collect and store player data responsibly, respecting their privacy and adhering to legal requirements.

2. **Bias and Misinterpretation**: Data analysis can be susceptible to bias and misinterpretation. It's essential to have skilled analysts who can draw accurate conclusions from the data.

3. **Maintaining Creativity**: Data should inform, not replace, creativity in game design. Striking a balance between data-driven decisions and creative innovation is crucial.

In conclusion, data-driven game design empowers developers to create more engaging and balanced games. By collecting and analyzing player behavior data, designers can make informed decisions that enhance gameplay, level design, and monetization strategies. However, it's essential to address ethical concerns and maintain a balance between data and creative intuition to deliver compelling gaming experiences.

Section 14.4: Balancing and Fine-Tuning Based on Analytics

Balancing and fine-tuning a game is a critical aspect of game development that can significantly impact the player's experience. In this section, we'll delve into how analytics can be used to identify and address balancing issues and provide insights into optimizing game mechanics.

The Importance of Game Balancing

Game balancing refers to the process of ensuring that different aspects of a game, such as characters, weapons, abilities, and resources, are adjusted to provide an enjoyable and fair experience for players. Balanced gameplay is essential for:

1. **Player Engagement**: A well-balanced game keeps players engaged and motivated. When challenges are appropriately balanced, players are more likely to stay committed to the game.

2. **Competitive Play**: In multiplayer games, balance is crucial to maintaining a competitive environment. Players should feel that victory or defeat depends on their skill and strategy rather than imbalances in the game.

3. **Longevity**: A balanced game has a longer lifespan. Players are more likely to continue playing and exploring when they encounter a well-tuned experience.

Using Analytics for Balancing

Analytics plays a vital role in identifying areas that require balancing adjustments:

1. **Player Data**: Collect data on player interactions, such as win/loss ratios, character or weapon usage, and gameplay progression.

2. **Heatmaps**: Analyze heatmaps to visualize player behavior within levels or maps. Heatmaps can reveal areas of the game where players struggle or excel.

3. **A/B Testing**: Conduct A/B tests by implementing different balance changes for separate player groups. Analyze which changes lead to improved player experiences.

4. **Feedback Analysis**: Incorporate player feedback into the balancing process. Player forums, surveys, and reviews can provide valuable insights into perceived imbalances.

Iterative Balancing

Balancing is rarely a one-time task; it's an iterative process throughout a game's development and post-launch phases:

1. **Pre-launch Balancing**: Before releasing the game, conduct thorough balance testing to address any glaring issues. This phase helps establish a baseline balance.

2. **Post-launch Balancing**: After the game is live, monitor player behavior and feedback. Continuously make adjustments to maintain or improve balance.

3. **DLC and Updates**: When releasing additional content, consider how it impacts the game's balance. Ensure that new characters, weapons, or features are well-integrated without disrupting the existing balance.

Examples of Balancing Adjustments

Let's explore a couple of examples of how analytics-driven balancing adjustments can improve a game:

Character Balance in a MOBA:
- Analytics show that a specific character has an exceptionally high win rate.
- Developers analyze gameplay data and discover that the character's abilities are overpowered.
- They make adjustments to the character's abilities, reducing their effectiveness.
- Subsequent data indicates improved character balance and a more diverse selection of characters in matches.

Weapon Balance in an FPS:
- Heatmaps reveal that a particular weapon is dominant in most matches.
- Designers analyze the weapon's statistics and find that it has a faster time-to-kill (TTK) than other weapons.
- They reduce the weapon's damage output and monitor its impact on gameplay.
- Players report a more balanced and enjoyable experience, with a wider variety of weapon choices.

While analytics-driven balancing is powerful, it comes with its own set of challenges and considerations:

1. **Player Perception**: Sometimes, player perception of balance differs from statistical analysis. Developers must strike a balance between data-driven decisions and player satisfaction.

2. **Data Quality**: The accuracy and relevance of the data collected are crucial. Incomplete or biased data can lead to incorrect balancing decisions.

3. **Over-balancing**: Overly frequent balancing adjustments can disrupt the player experience. Strive for a balance between regular updates and maintaining game stability.

In summary, analytics-driven balancing is a fundamental aspect of game development that ensures players have an enjoyable and fair experience. By collecting and analyzing player data, developers can identify and address balancing issues, leading to more engaging and competitive games. However, developers must also consider player perception and maintain a healthy balance between data-driven decisions and player satisfaction.

Section 14.5: Ethical Considerations in Player Data Collection

As the game development industry continues to evolve, the collection and utilization of player data have become increasingly prevalent. However, with this rise in data-driven decision-making comes a responsibility to handle player data ethically and transparently. In this section, we'll explore the ethical considerations that game developers should keep in mind when collecting and using player data.

Transparency and Informed Consent

One of the core principles of ethical data collection is transparency. Game developers should be open and clear about the types of data they collect, how it will be used, and who will have access to it. This information should be easily accessible to players, typically through a privacy policy or terms of service agreement.

Informed consent is another essential aspect. Players should have the option to consent or decline data collection. Consent should be freely given, meaning that players shouldn't be forced to share their data as a condition of playing the game. Providing clear choices and respecting players' decisions is crucial.

Data Minimization

Data minimization is a principle that emphasizes collecting only the data necessary for a specific purpose. Game developers should avoid collecting excessive or irrelevant data about players. By minimizing data collection, developers can reduce the risk of privacy breaches and ensure that players' personal information is handled with care.

Data Security and Protection

Protecting player data is paramount. Game developers must implement robust security measures to safeguard against data breaches or unauthorized access. This includes encrypting sensitive data, regularly updating security protocols, and educating team members on best practices for data protection.

In the event of a data breach, developers should have a response plan in place to mitigate the impact on players and comply with relevant data protection laws, such as the General Data Protection Regulation (GDPR) in Europe.

Anonymization and De-identification

When collecting player data, developers should consider methods for anonymizing or de-identifying data. Anonymization involves removing personally identifiable information (PII) from data sets, making it challenging to trace data back to individual players. De-identification involves replacing or altering PII to protect player privacy.

Data Retention Policies

Developers should establish clear data retention policies that specify how long player data will be stored. Retaining data for longer than necessary can pose privacy risks. By defining retention periods and deleting data when it's no longer needed, developers can reduce the risk of data misuse.

Third-Party Services and Partnerships

Many games use third-party services for analytics, advertising, or other functionalities. Game developers must be transparent about these partnerships and inform players about the third-party services used. Players should have the option to opt out of data sharing with these services if they wish.

Inclusive and Ethical Design

Ethical considerations should extend to the design of the game itself. Developers should avoid designing mechanics that exploit addictive behaviors or encourage excessive in-game purchases. Balancing the revenue-generating aspects of a game with ethical considerations is crucial for maintaining player trust.

Regular Audits and Compliance

To ensure ongoing ethical data practices, developers should conduct regular audits of their data collection and usage procedures. This includes monitoring compliance with relevant data protection laws and staying informed about evolving regulations.

Ethical data collection and usage are essential for building trust with players and protecting their privacy. Game developers must prioritize transparency, consent, data minimization, security, and responsible data practices throughout a game's development and post-launch phases. By adhering to ethical standards, developers can create a safer and more trustworthy gaming environment for players.

Chapter 15: Advanced Marketing and Monetization Strategies

Section 15.1: Marketing Techniques for Advanced Game Developers

In the competitive world of game development, effective marketing is often the key to success. While marketing is a broad and dynamic field, this section will focus on advanced marketing techniques tailored to experienced game developers looking to maximize their game's visibility and impact.

1. Data-Driven Marketing

Data-driven marketing leverages analytics and player data to make informed decisions. Advanced developers utilize player behavior data to refine their marketing strategies. This includes analyzing player demographics, engagement patterns, and conversion rates. By understanding their audience better, developers can create more targeted and personalized marketing campaigns.

2. Influencer Marketing

Influencer marketing has become a powerful tool for promoting games. Experienced developers collaborate with relevant influencers and content creators in the gaming industry. These partnerships can lead to increased exposure and credibility. However, selecting the right influencers who align with the game's genre and target audience is crucial.

3. Community Building and Engagement

Establishing and nurturing a dedicated community around your game is essential. Advanced developers create official forums, Discord servers, or social media groups where players can connect, share experiences, and provide feedback. Engaging with the community not only builds a loyal player base but also generates valuable user-generated content for marketing.

4. Pre-Launch Hype Campaigns

Building anticipation before a game's launch is an art form. Developers tease their audience with trailers, teasers, and behind-the-scenes content. Creating a buzz and generating excitement can lead to a successful launch day. Advanced developers carefully plan and execute these campaigns, often involving countdowns, exclusive rewards, and limited-time offers.

5. A/B Testing and Iteration

Advanced developers employ A/B testing to refine marketing materials continually. By testing different ad creatives, landing pages, or call-to-action buttons, they can identify what resonates best with their audience. This iterative approach ensures that marketing efforts are continually optimized for maximum effectiveness.

6. Cross-Promotion and Partnerships

Collaborating with other game developers for cross-promotion can expand your game's reach. This can involve in-game partnerships, where players from one game can access content or discounts in another. Strategic partnerships with non-competing but complementary games can be mutually beneficial.

7. App Store Optimization (ASO)

For mobile game developers, ASO is crucial for improving visibility on app stores. Advanced developers optimize their app store listings with relevant keywords, appealing visuals, and compelling descriptions. Regularly updating the game with new features and content also boosts rankings.

8. Retention Marketing

Keeping existing players engaged and coming back is often more cost-effective than acquiring new ones. Advanced developers implement retention marketing strategies, such as sending personalized emails, offering in-game rewards, or hosting special events for long-time players.

9. User-Generated Content (UGC) Campaigns

Encouraging players to create and share their content related to the game can lead to viral marketing. Developers organize UGC contests, challenges, or events where players can showcase their creativity. Sharing UGC on official channels further amplifies its reach.

10. Data Privacy and Compliance

In an era of heightened data privacy concerns, advanced developers prioritize compliance with regulations like GDPR and CCPA. They ensure that their marketing practices are transparent, and player data is handled with care, building trust among players.

Conclusion

Advanced marketing techniques are essential for game developers looking to stand out in a competitive market. These strategies involve a deep understanding of player data, community building, influencer collaborations, and ethical marketing practices. By mastering these techniques, experienced developers can maximize their game's success and player engagement.

Section 15.2: Developing and Implementing Monetization Models

Monetization is a critical aspect of game development, allowing developers to generate revenue from their creations. In this section, we'll explore advanced strategies for developing and implementing monetization models that can help sustain and grow your game development endeavors.

1. Diverse Monetization Models

Experienced game developers understand the importance of diversifying monetization models. Rather than relying solely on a single revenue stream, they implement a combination of models. These may include:

- **In-App Purchases (IAPs):** Offering virtual goods, currency, or upgrades for real money.
- **Advertising:** Incorporating ads, such as banners, interstitials, or rewarded videos, within the game.
- **Subscription Services:** Providing players with premium access, content, or features through subscription plans.
- **DLCs and Expansions:** Releasing downloadable content or expansions that extend the game's content.
- **Cosmetic Items:** Selling purely cosmetic items, such as skins, costumes, or emotes, that don't affect gameplay.
- **Loot Boxes:** Implementing randomized loot box systems, often with rare items or characters.
- **Season Passes:** Offering access to a series of updates or content releases for a fixed price.

2. Player-Centric Approach

Successful monetization models prioritize the player's experience. Developers must strike a balance between generating revenue and ensuring that players don't feel pressured or exploited. Advanced developers implement player-centric strategies by:

- **Avoiding Pay-to-Win (P2W):** Steering clear of mechanics that grant paying players significant advantages over non-paying ones.
- **Providing Value:** Ensuring that any paid content or features offer genuine value and enhance the gameplay experience.
- **Fair Pricing:** Setting reasonable prices for in-game items and subscriptions, avoiding excessive costs.
- **Opt-In Advertising:** Allowing players to opt into watching ads for rewards rather than forcing them.
- **Transparency:** Clearly communicating how monetization works within the game, including rates and odds for loot boxes.

3. Live Operations and Events

Advanced developers keep players engaged through live operations and special events. These events introduce limited-time content, challenges, or rewards, encouraging players to log in regularly. Special events can include holiday-themed content, tournaments, or community challenges. These events create a sense of urgency and excitement, driving player engagement and monetization.

4. Analyzing Player Behavior

Advanced monetization strategies heavily rely on data analysis. Developers use player behavior analytics to understand how players interact with the game and its monetization elements. By tracking player spending habits, engagement patterns, and drop-off points, developers can make informed adjustments to their monetization models.

5. Personalization and Targeting

Personalization is a key component of advanced monetization. Developers employ algorithms that tailor offers and recommendations to individual player preferences. This level of personalization increases the likelihood of players making in-game purchases. However, developers must handle player data responsibly and ensure compliance with privacy regulations.

6. Seasonal and Limited-Time Offers

To create a sense of urgency and drive monetization, developers introduce seasonal or limited-time offers. These can include exclusive items or discounts available for a short period. Players who fear missing out are more likely to make purchases during these windows.

7. Regular Content Updates

Regularly updating the game with new content, features, or events keeps players engaged and encourages them to spend. Developers plan and communicate a content roadmap to maintain player interest and monetization momentum.

8. Ethical Considerations

Ethical considerations play a significant role in advanced monetization. Developers should avoid exploiting addictive tendencies, especially in younger players. They must also consider the impact of monetization on player well-being and mental health.

Conclusion

Developing and implementing advanced monetization models requires a deep understanding of player behavior, ethical considerations, and a commitment to providing value to players. Successful developers prioritize player experience while leveraging diverse monetization strategies to sustain and grow their games. Monetization should be seen as a means to support ongoing game development and provide players with a rewarding experience.

Section 15.3: Building and Maintaining a Loyal Player Base

Building and maintaining a loyal player base is a critical aspect of long-term success in the game development industry. In this section, we'll explore strategies and practices that advanced developers use to foster player loyalty, encourage player retention, and create a dedicated community around their games.

1. Player-Centric Design

Player-centric design is at the core of building a loyal player base. Advanced developers prioritize creating games that cater to the needs, preferences, and desires of their target audience. This involves:

- **Player Feedback:** Actively seeking and listening to player feedback to make informed design decisions and improvements.
- **User Experience (UX) Optimization:** Ensuring that the game provides a smooth, enjoyable, and intuitive experience for players.
- **Regular Updates:** Continuously improving and expanding the game based on player input and emerging trends.

2. Community Engagement

Community engagement is a powerful tool for building loyalty. Developers establish and maintain communication channels with their player base, including forums, social media, and official websites. They:

- **Interact Actively:** Engage with players through forums, social media, live streams, and Q&A sessions.
- **Transparency:** Share development updates, patch notes, and future plans to keep players informed.
- **Events and Contests:** Organize community events, contests, and tournaments to foster a sense of belonging and competition.
- **Feedback Loops:** Encourage and reward players for contributing to the game's development by reporting bugs, suggesting improvements, or creating user-generated content.

3. Player Support and Communication

Providing exceptional player support is essential. Advanced developers ensure that players can easily reach out for assistance and that their concerns are promptly addressed. This includes:

- **Dedicated Support Team:** Having a dedicated support team to respond to player inquiries and issues.
- **In-Game Support Features:** Integrating in-game tools for reporting bugs, providing feedback, and seeking assistance.
- **Prompt Responses:** Responding to player concerns and issues in a timely and empathetic manner.

4. Regular Content Updates

Regularly updating the game with fresh content, features, and improvements keeps players engaged. Advanced developers plan and execute content updates on a consistent schedule. These updates could include:

- **New Levels or Maps:** Expanding the game world with new environments for exploration.
- **Additional Characters or Heroes:** Introducing new playable characters or heroes to diversify gameplay.
- **Events and Challenges:** Launching limited-time events, challenges, and seasonal content.
- **Balancing and Gameplay Tweaks:** Making adjustments to ensure a fair and enjoyable gaming experience.

5. Community-Driven Development

Community-driven development involves collaborating with the player base to shape the game's future. Developers invite players to participate in the decision-making process regarding game features, changes, and improvements. This sense of ownership fosters player loyalty.

6. Exclusive Rewards and Perks

Rewarding player loyalty with exclusive in-game items, cosmetics, or access to premium content can incentivize players to stay engaged. These rewards could be given to long-term players, contributors to the community, or participants in special events.

7. Evolving with Player Needs

Advanced developers remain flexible and adaptive. They monitor player trends, preferences, and technology advancements to ensure their games evolve to meet changing player needs. This may involve porting the game to new platforms, introducing cross-play features, or embracing emerging technologies.

8. Ethical Considerations

Ethical considerations remain paramount when building a loyal player base. Developers must prioritize player well-being, avoid exploitative practices, and ensure a safe and inclusive gaming environment. Ethical practices not only build loyalty but also contribute to a positive reputation in the gaming community.

Conclusion

Building and maintaining a loyal player base requires a commitment to player-centric design, transparent communication, and ongoing support. Advanced developers recognize that player loyalty is not just about retaining players but also about fostering a passionate and engaged community that continues to grow and support the game over time.

Section 15.4: Crowdfunding and Community Support Models

Crowdfunding has become a viable way for advanced game developers to secure funding and engage with their player base simultaneously. In this section, we'll explore how developers leverage crowdfunding platforms and community support models to finance their projects and build a dedicated fanbase.

1. Crowdfunding Platforms

Several crowdfunding platforms, such as Kickstarter, Indiegogo, and Fig, have become popular choices for game developers seeking funding. Advanced developers utilize these platforms strategically:

- **Campaign Planning:** Developers plan comprehensive crowdfunding campaigns with detailed information about the game's concept, gameplay, and development progress.
- **Engaging Campaign Page:** Creating a visually appealing and informative campaign page is crucial. Developers use videos, concept art, and gameplay snippets to attract potential backers.
- **Reward Tiers:** Developers offer enticing reward tiers that range from early access to exclusive in-game content, physical merchandise, and even credits in the game.
- **Regular Updates:** Keeping backers informed through regular updates during the campaign and development phase builds trust and maintains interest.

2. Community Building

Building a strong community around the game is essential for successful crowdfunding and long-term support. Developers use various tactics to cultivate a supportive fanbase:

- **Social Media Presence:** Establishing a robust presence on platforms like Twitter, Facebook, Reddit, and Discord allows developers to connect with potential backers and fans.
- **Dev Blogs and Newsletters:** Developers maintain developer blogs and newsletters to provide deeper insights into the game's progress, development challenges, and behind-the-scenes content.
- **Engaging with Fans:** Actively engaging with fans through Q&A sessions, polls, and discussions ensures a sense of involvement and investment in the project.
- **Transparency:** Developers maintain transparency about the game's development, including any setbacks or delays, to maintain trust within the community.

3. Stretch Goals

Developers often use stretch goals to incentivize additional funding beyond the initial target. These goals can include extra features, expanded content, or ports to additional platforms. This not only encourages backers to increase their pledges but also enhances the overall value proposition of the campaign.

4. Backer Feedback and Collaboration

Advanced developers value the input of their backers and involve them in key decisions. Backer feedback can shape the direction of the game, from gameplay mechanics to art style. This collaboration fosters a sense of ownership and loyalty among backers.

5. Post-Campaign Engagement

After a successful crowdfunding campaign, developers maintain engagement with backers. They provide regular updates on the game's development, share exclusive content, and keep backers informed about milestones and release dates.

6. Managing Expectations

Managing expectations is crucial in crowdfunding. Developers are transparent about potential risks and challenges, setting realistic delivery dates, and openly communicating any delays or changes in project scope. This ensures that backers remain supportive and understanding.

7. Community Support Models

In addition to crowdfunding, some developers employ community support models. These models can include:

- **Patreon:** Developers offer exclusive content and perks to patrons who support them on a monthly basis, creating a sustainable income stream.
- **Early Access:** Developers release early versions of their games to a select group of players, allowing them to playtest and provide feedback before the official launch.
- **User-Generated Content:** Enabling players to create and share their content within the game fosters a dedicated community and encourages ongoing engagement.

Conclusion

Crowdfunding and community support models offer advanced game developers the opportunity to secure funding and build an enthusiastic fanbase simultaneously. However, success in these endeavors requires careful planning, community engagement, and a commitment to transparency and communication. When executed effectively, these models can lead to the development of outstanding games with passionate and dedicated communities.

Section 15.5: Post-Launch Strategies: DLCs, Updates, and Community Management

Successful post-launch strategies are essential for sustaining a game's lifespan, keeping players engaged, and maximizing revenue. In this section, we'll delve into the various aspects of post-launch strategies, including downloadable content (DLCs), updates, and community management.

1. Downloadable Content (DLCs)

Downloadable content is a common post-launch strategy to extend a game's content and monetize it further. Advanced developers carefully plan and execute DLCs:

- **Content Variety:** DLCs should offer diverse content, such as new story arcs, characters, levels, cosmetics, or gameplay modes, to cater to different player preferences.
- **Quality Assurance:** Maintaining the quality and polish of DLCs is crucial to meet player expectations and uphold the game's reputation.
- **Pricing Strategy:** Developers consider pricing options, including season passes, individual purchases, or bundles, to maximize revenue while providing value to players.
- **Communication:** Clear communication about upcoming DLCs, their features, and release dates keeps players engaged and informed.
- **Balancing Gameplay:** Developers ensure that DLC content doesn't disrupt the game's balance or create a pay-to-win scenario, which can harm the player experience.

2. Updates and Patches

Regular updates and patches are vital for addressing bugs, improving gameplay, and maintaining player interest. Advanced developers focus on the following:

- **Player Feedback:** Actively gather and listen to player feedback to identify issues, concerns, and areas for improvement.
- **Bug Fixes:** Quickly address critical bugs and issues that affect gameplay, performance, or stability.
- **Balance Tweaks:** Continuously evaluate and adjust game balance based on data and player feedback to ensure fairness.
- **Feature Additions:** Introduce new features, quality-of-life improvements, or requested enhancements to enhance the player experience.
- **Community Involvement:** Acknowledge and credit players who contribute to identifying and fixing bugs, fostering a sense of community involvement.

3. Live Events and Seasons

Live events and seasonal content can keep players engaged and returning to the game. Developers utilize the following strategies:

- **Timely Events:** Plan and schedule in-game events, challenges, and themed seasons to coincide with real-world holidays or events.
- **Exclusive Rewards:** Offer exclusive in-game rewards, cosmetics, or limited-time content during events to incentivize participation.
- **Community Challenges:** Create collaborative community challenges that encourage players to work together to achieve common goals.

4. Community Management

Effective community management is essential for maintaining a positive player community and addressing player concerns:

- **Moderation:** Enforce clear community guidelines and moderate forums, social media, and in-game chat to prevent toxic behavior.
- **Direct Communication:** Maintain open lines of communication with the player community through forums, social media channels, and regular developer updates.
- **Feedback Channels:** Provide dedicated channels for players to submit feedback, bug reports, and suggestions, and acknowledge their contributions.

5. Player Support

Providing excellent player support is crucial for retaining players and resolving issues promptly:

- **Customer Support:** Offer responsive customer support to address player inquiries, technical issues, and account problems.
- **Knowledge Base:** Maintain a comprehensive knowledge base or FAQ section to help players troubleshoot common problems independently.
- **Feedback Loop:** Use player support interactions to identify recurring issues and prioritize them for resolution in future updates.

6. Data-Driven Decisions

Advanced developers rely on player data and analytics to inform post-launch strategies:

- **Player Behavior Analysis:** Analyze player behavior data to understand player preferences, engagement patterns, and pain points.
- **A/B Testing:** Conduct A/B tests to assess the impact of potential changes or features on player retention and monetization.
- **Iterative Development:** Iterate on post-launch strategies based on data insights to continuously improve the game's performance and player experience.

Conclusion

Post-launch strategies are integral to the long-term success of advanced games. By carefully planning and executing DLCs, updates, live events, and effective community management, developers can maintain player engagement, drive revenue, and foster a dedicated player community. Data-driven decision-making ensures that strategies are aligned with player preferences and evolving industry trends, ultimately contributing to a thriving and sustainable game ecosystem.

Chapter 16: CryEngine Community and Collaboration

Section 16.1: Engaging with the CryEngine Developer Community

Engaging with the CryEngine developer community is a crucial aspect of your journey as a game developer. CryEngine, like many other game development ecosystems, has a vibrant and active community of developers, artists, designers, and enthusiasts. In this section, we will explore the various ways you can engage with this community and leverage it to enhance your skills and projects.

The Value of Community

The CryEngine community offers a wealth of knowledge, experience, and resources that can be immensely valuable to you. Whether you are a seasoned developer or just starting, interacting with the community can help you in several ways:

1. **Learning and Sharing:** Engaging with others allows you to learn from their experiences and share your own knowledge. This exchange of information can lead to insights and solutions you might not have discovered on your own.

2. **Networking:** Building connections within the community can open doors to collaborations, job opportunities, and mentorship. Networking is essential for personal and professional growth.

3. **Getting Help:** When you encounter challenges or problems in your projects, the community can be a valuable source of help and guidance. Many developers are willing to assist with technical issues or provide feedback on your work.

4. **Staying Updated:** The CryEngine community is often the first to know about updates, plugins, and tools related to the engine. By staying connected, you can ensure that you are up-to-date with the latest developments.

Online Forums and Communities

One of the primary ways to engage with the CryEngine community is through online forums and communities. Websites like the CryEngine forums, Reddit's CryEngine subreddit, and CryDev.net are popular platforms where developers discuss various topics related to CryEngine development. Here are some tips for effectively using these platforms:

- **Ask Questions:** Don't hesitate to ask questions when you're stuck on a problem or need advice. Be clear and specific in your questions to receive helpful responses.

- **Contribute:** If you have expertise in a particular area, consider contributing to discussions and helping others. Sharing your knowledge can establish your reputation within the community.

- **Follow Guidelines:** Each platform may have its own rules and guidelines. Familiarize yourself with these guidelines to ensure a positive and respectful interaction with the community.

Collaborative Projects

Collaborative projects are an excellent way to connect with fellow CryEngine developers and gain practical experience. Many developers in the community work on open-source projects or participate in group endeavors. You can find such projects on platforms like GitHub and collaborate on game development, plugins, and tools.

Attend Conferences and Meetups

While online interactions are valuable, attending CryEngine-related conferences and local meetups can provide in-person networking opportunities. Keep an eye out for events, conferences, and meetups related to CryEngine in your area or online. These gatherings are an excellent way to meet like-minded individuals, share experiences, and learn from experts.

Share Your Work

Don't be shy about sharing your CryEngine projects with the community. Whether it's a game prototype, a plugin, or a tutorial, sharing your work can lead to valuable feedback and recognition. Platforms like the CryEngine Marketplace and community forums are great places to showcase your creations.

In conclusion, engaging with the CryEngine developer community can significantly enhance your skills, knowledge, and career opportunities. It's a supportive and collaborative environment where you can learn, share, and grow as a game developer. So, dive in, participate actively, and make the most of this vibrant community!

Section 16.2: Collaborative Projects and Open Source Contributions

Collaborative projects and open source contributions are essential aspects of engaging with the CryEngine community. These initiatives offer opportunities to work with other developers, contribute to shared goals, and showcase your skills. In this section, we will explore the benefits of participating in collaborative projects and contributing to open source efforts within the CryEngine ecosystem.

The Value of Collaboration

Collaborative projects involve working together with other developers to create games, tools, or plugins. These endeavors come with several advantages:

1. **Skill Enhancement:** Collaborating on projects exposes you to a variety of challenges and solutions. You can learn from others, acquire new skills, and gain hands-on experience in a team setting.

2. **Networking:** Collaborators often become valuable connections in your professional network. Building relationships with fellow developers can lead to future job opportunities and partnerships.

3. **Portfolio Building:** Contributions to collaborative projects can be added to your portfolio, showcasing your abilities and commitment to potential employers or clients.

4. **Shared Resources:** Teams pool their resources, such as code libraries, assets, and knowledge, to achieve common goals more efficiently.

Finding Collaborative Projects

There are several avenues to discover and join collaborative CryEngine projects:

Online Forums and Communities

CryEngine-related online forums and communities, such as the CryEngine forums and Reddit's CryEngine subreddit, often feature announcements and recruitment posts for collaborative projects. Keep an eye on these platforms to find opportunities that match your interests and skills.

GitHub and GitLab

Platforms like GitHub and GitLab host many open source CryEngine projects. You can explore repositories, contribute to ongoing projects, or even start your own. Collaborative coding and version control tools make it easy to work with others remotely.

Game Jams

Participating in game jams is an excellent way to engage in short-term collaborative projects. Game jam events typically have themes and time constraints, fostering creativity and teamwork. The CryEngine community occasionally organizes or participates in game jams, which can be a fun and educational experience.

Contributing to Open Source

Open source contributions involve actively participating in the development of open source CryEngine projects. By contributing to open source projects, you can:

- **Improve the Engine:** Help enhance the CryEngine by fixing bugs, implementing new features, or optimizing existing ones.

- **Extend Functionality:** Contribute plugins, tools, or assets that benefit the community and extend the engine's capabilities.

- **Gain Recognition:** Establishing yourself as a contributor to open source projects can boost your professional reputation within the CryEngine community and beyond.

When participating in collaborative projects or open source contributions, consider the following best practices:

- **Communication:** Maintain clear and open communication with your collaborators. Use project management tools, chat platforms, or video calls to stay in touch.

- **Version Control:** Utilize version control systems like Git to track changes and manage project files. Ensure you are familiar with branching, merging, and resolving conflicts.

- **Documentation:** Write documentation for your contributions, making it easier for others to understand and use your work.

- **Respect Licenses:** Respect the licensing terms of open source projects and ensure you comply with their requirements.

- **Give Credit:** Properly attribute your collaborators and credit the original authors of open source projects.

In conclusion, collaborating on projects and contributing to open source initiatives within the CryEngine community can be a rewarding experience. It offers opportunities for skill development, networking, and portfolio enhancement while contributing to the growth of the CryEngine ecosystem. Embrace collaboration, share your expertise, and become an active member of this thriving developer community.

Section 16.3: Networking and Mentorship in the CryEngine Ecosystem

Networking and mentorship are invaluable aspects of your journey within the CryEngine ecosystem. In this section, we'll explore the significance of networking, finding mentors, and becoming a mentor to foster your growth as a CryEngine developer.

The Power of Networking

Networking involves establishing and nurturing relationships with other developers, professionals, and enthusiasts in the CryEngine community. Effective networking offers numerous advantages:

1. **Knowledge Exchange:** Networking provides opportunities to exchange ideas, share experiences, and learn from others in the field. You can gain insights into best practices, problem-solving techniques, and innovative approaches.

2. **Collaboration:** Building a network of contacts can lead to collaborative projects, partnerships, and job opportunities. Many developers find their next project or job through their network.

3. **Mentorship:** Networking can connect you with experienced mentors who can guide your development journey. Mentors can offer advice, review your work, and help you overcome challenges.

4. **Visibility:** Actively participating in the CryEngine community can make you more visible to potential employers, collaborators, and clients. Your reputation and contributions can open doors to exciting opportunities.

Finding Mentors

Mentors play a crucial role in your professional growth. They can provide guidance, feedback, and valuable insights. Here's how to find mentors within the CryEngine community:

Online Communities

Participate in CryEngine-related online forums, social media groups, and Discord servers. Engage in discussions, ask for advice, and connect with experienced developers who may be willing to mentor you.

Game Development Events

Attend conferences, workshops, and game development events where you can meet industry professionals and potential mentors. Events like GDC (Game Developers Conference) often feature experienced CryEngine developers.

Mentorship Programs

Some organizations and communities offer mentorship programs for aspiring game developers. Research such programs and apply to be paired with a mentor who specializes in CryEngine development.

Becoming a Mentor

Mentoring is a two-way street, and as you gain experience, consider becoming a mentor yourself. Here are the benefits of mentoring others:

- **Solidify Knowledge:** Teaching others reinforces your own understanding and expertise.

- **Pay It Forward:** Mentoring allows you to give back to the community and support the next generation of developers.

- **Networking:** As a mentor, you can expand your network and collaborate with talented individuals you help guide.

- **Personal Growth:** Mentoring enhances your communication, leadership, and coaching skills.

Online Tutorials and Workshops

Create tutorials, write articles, or host online workshops related to CryEngine development. Sharing your knowledge in this way can help others learn and improve their skills.

Community Involvement

Actively participate in CryEngine forums, Discord servers, and social media groups. Answer questions, provide guidance, and engage with those seeking assistance. This not only helps others but also enhances your visibility within the community.

Local or Virtual Meetups

Consider organizing or participating in local or virtual CryEngine developer meetups. These events provide opportunities to connect with developers in your area or worldwide and share your expertise.

Best Practices for Networking and Mentorship

When networking and engaging in mentorship, keep the following best practices in mind:

- **Be Respectful:** Show respect for others' time, opinions, and expertise. Be polite and considerate in your interactions.

- **Follow Up:** Maintain ongoing connections with your network. Follow up with contacts, share your progress, and express gratitude.

- **Give as Much as You Receive:** If you receive mentorship, consider mentoring others in return. The cycle of knowledge sharing benefits the entire community.

- **Seek Diverse Perspectives:** Connect with individuals from diverse backgrounds and experiences. Different perspectives can lead to innovative solutions and broaden your horizons.

In conclusion, networking and mentorship are vital components of success within the CryEngine community. Building a strong network and engaging in mentorship relationships can accelerate your growth as a developer, open doors to exciting opportunities, and contribute to the thriving ecosystem of CryEngine developers. Embrace the power of connections, both as a learner and a mentor, and watch your skills and career flourish.

Section 16.4: Participating in Game Jams and Competitions

Participating in game jams and competitions is an exciting and valuable way to enhance your skills, showcase your creativity, and connect with the CryEngine community. In this section, we'll explore the benefits of game jams and competitions and provide tips on how to make the most of these events.

The Significance of Game Jams and Competitions

Game jams and competitions offer several advantages for CryEngine developers:

1. **Skill Development:** These events provide an opportunity to challenge yourself, learn new techniques, and improve your problem-solving abilities. You'll often need to work with time constraints, which can boost your efficiency.

2. **Portfolio Enhancement:** Creating a game during a jam or competition can add impressive projects to your portfolio. High-quality CryEngine work from such events can catch the eye of potential employers or collaborators.

3. **Community Engagement:** Game jams and competitions bring together developers, artists, designers, and enthusiasts. Engaging with others in the CryEngine community fosters networking and collaboration.

4. **Feedback and Exposure:** You'll receive feedback from peers and judges, helping you refine your skills. Winning or placing well can also bring recognition and exposure to your work.

Tips for Successful Participation

Here are some tips to make the most of your participation in game jams and competitions:

1. Choose the Right Events

Select game jams and competitions that align with your interests and skill level. Some events have specific themes or limitations, so read the rules and guidelines carefully.

2. Plan Efficiently

Time is often limited in these events, so plan your game concept and development approach wisely. Prioritize essential features and avoid overly ambitious ideas.

3. Collaborate

Consider forming or joining a team. Collaborating with others can bring diverse skills and ideas to your project and make development more manageable.

4. Focus on Innovation

Game jams encourage creativity and experimentation. Don't be afraid to try unconventional ideas or explore unique gameplay mechanics.

5. Documentation

Keep a development diary or document your progress. This documentation can help you organize your thoughts, track your decisions, and create a post-mortem analysis after the event.

6. Seek Feedback

Engage with other participants during the event. Share your work for feedback and offer feedback to others. Constructive criticism can help you refine your game.

7. Time Management

Efficient time management is crucial. Allocate time for brainstorming, development, testing, and polishing. Avoid last-minute rushes that can lead to errors.

8. Playtest

Regularly playtest your game to identify and fix issues. Invite others to playtest as well, as fresh perspectives can uncover hidden problems.

9. Submission

Ensure you follow the submission guidelines precisely. Missing deadlines or failing to meet submission requirements can disqualify your entry.

10. Post-Event Reflection

After the event, take time to reflect on your experience. Consider what went well and what could be improved in future projects.

Popular Game Jams and Competitions

Several game jams and competitions cater to CryEngine developers and game creators in general. Here are a few popular ones:

- **Global Game Jam:** A worldwide event where participants create games over a weekend based on a common theme.

- **Ludum Dare:** Known for its strict 48-hour development period, Ludum Dare challenges developers to create games from scratch.

- **CryEngine Indie Game Development Contest:** Crytek occasionally hosts contests specifically for CryEngine developers, offering cash prizes and recognition.

- **Unreal Engine and Unity Game Jams:** While not CryEngine-specific, these engines host frequent game jams that welcome developers from various backgrounds.

Participating in these events can be a thrilling and educational experience, whether you're a beginner or an experienced developer. Game jams and competitions push your creative boundaries, introduce you to new ideas, and allow you to showcase your talents to a wider audience. So, embrace the challenge, have fun, and let your imagination run wild in the world of game development.

Section 16.5: Sharing Knowledge: Tutorials and Workshops

Sharing knowledge through tutorials and workshops is a valuable way to contribute to the CryEngine community while enhancing your own expertise. In this section, we'll explore the benefits of creating tutorials and hosting workshops and provide guidance on how to effectively share your knowledge with others.

The Significance of Tutorials and Workshops

Tutorials and workshops play a crucial role in the CryEngine ecosystem for several reasons:

1. **Community Building:** Creating tutorials and hosting workshops fosters a sense of community among CryEngine developers. It encourages collaboration and knowledge exchange.

2. **Skill Development:** Preparing educational content requires a deep understanding of CryEngine concepts. By teaching others, you reinforce your own knowledge and expertise.

3. **Resource Availability:** Well-documented tutorials and workshops serve as valuable resources for developers at all levels. They can help newcomers get started and offer advanced insights for experienced users.

4. **Recognition:** Sharing your knowledge can lead to recognition within the CryEngine community. You may become known as an expert in your field, which can open doors for collaboration and career opportunities.

Tips for Creating Tutorials and Hosting Workshops

Here are some tips to help you create effective tutorials and host engaging workshops:

1. Choose Topics Wisely

Select topics that you are passionate about and have expertise in. Consider the needs and interests of your target audience when deciding what to cover.

2. Plan Your Content

Create a structured outline or lesson plan for your tutorial or workshop. Clearly define your learning objectives and the key points you want to convey.

3. Be Clear and Concise

Ensure that your explanations are clear and easy to understand. Avoid jargon and use plain language to explain complex concepts.

4. Provide Examples

Use practical examples, code snippets, and demonstrations to illustrate your points. Visual aids and hands-on exercises can enhance the learning experience.

5. Interactivity

Engage your audience through interactive elements. Encourage questions and discussions during workshops, and provide opportunities for participants to apply what they've learned.

6. Use Multiple Formats

Consider using a variety of formats for your tutorials and workshops, such as written guides, video tutorials, live webinars, or in-person sessions. Different learners have different preferences.

7. Document Your Content

Ensure that your tutorials and workshop materials are well-documented and easily accessible. Provide downloadable resources, code samples, and reference materials.

8. Encourage Feedback

Invite feedback from your audience to improve your content. Constructive criticism can help you refine your teaching methods and address any gaps in your tutorials or workshops.

9. Keep It Updated

CryEngine and game development technologies evolve over time. Regularly update your tutorials and workshops to reflect the latest best practices and features.

10. Promote Your Content

Share your tutorials and workshop announcements on CryEngine forums, social media, and relevant communities. Building an audience takes time, so be patient and consistent.

Hosting Workshops

If you plan to host workshops, consider these additional tips:

- Choose a platform for hosting virtual workshops, such as Zoom, Microsoft Teams, or Discord.
- Provide clear instructions on how participants can join and participate in your workshop.

- Test your setup, including audio and video quality, before the workshop.
- Record your workshops for future reference and to reach a wider audience.

CryEngine developers often seek tutorials and workshops on various topics. Here are some popular areas of interest:

- **Level Design Techniques:** Covering topics like terrain creation, asset placement, and environmental storytelling.

- **Scripting and Gameplay Mechanics:** Explaining how to create custom gameplay elements using Lua or C++.

- **Asset Creation and Animation:** Tutorials on modeling, rigging, animation, and character creation.

- **Performance Optimization:** Providing tips on optimizing CryEngine projects for better performance.

- **Multiplayer and Networking:** Demonstrating how to implement multiplayer features and networking solutions.

- **Advanced Rendering:** Covering shader programming, visual effects, and real-time global illumination.

By sharing your expertise in these areas or any other CryEngine-related topics, you can contribute to the growth and knowledge-sharing within the community while advancing your own skills and reputation. Remember that teaching is a two-way street, and you can learn as much from your audience as they can from you. So, embrace the opportunity to share knowledge and be an active participant in the CryEngine community.

Chapter 17: Future Technologies and CryEngine

Section 17.1: Emerging Technologies in Game Development

The world of game development is constantly evolving, driven by advancements in technology and the ever-changing demands of players. In this section, we'll explore the emerging technologies that are shaping the future of the gaming industry and their relevance to CryEngine.

The Dynamic Landscape of Game Development

Game development has come a long way since the early days of 2D pixel art and rudimentary physics simulations. Today, it's a multi-billion-dollar industry that encompasses a wide range of platforms, genres, and player experiences. Emerging technologies are a driving force behind this transformation, and they offer exciting opportunities for both developers and players.

Virtual Reality (VR) and Augmented Reality (AR)

One of the most notable advancements in recent years is the rise of VR and AR technologies. VR immerses players in entirely virtual worlds, while AR blends digital elements with the real world. CryEngine has embraced these technologies, allowing developers to create immersive VR and AR experiences. Whether it's exploring a fantasy realm in VR or overlaying digital information onto the physical world through AR, these technologies are revolutionizing how we interact with games.

Ray Tracing and Realistic Graphics

Real-time ray tracing has been a game-changer in terms of graphics quality. It enables the simulation of realistic lighting, reflections, and shadows, significantly enhancing visual fidelity. CryEngine has integrated ray tracing capabilities, making it possible to create stunningly realistic environments. As hardware becomes more powerful and affordable, ray tracing will become a standard feature in many games.

Cloud Gaming and Streaming

Cloud gaming services are on the rise, allowing players to stream games directly from remote servers. CryEngine's scalability makes it well-suited for cloud gaming, enabling developers to reach a broader audience without hardware limitations. As internet infrastructure improves, cloud gaming will become more accessible and offer high-quality gaming experiences on various devices.

Artificial Intelligence (AI) Advancements

AI is evolving rapidly, and it's not limited to just enemy behavior in games. Advanced AI can generate procedural content, adapt to player actions, and enhance overall game immersion. CryEngine's AI capabilities continue to evolve, making it easier for developers to create intelligent NPCs and dynamic game worlds.

Blockchain and NFT Integration

Blockchain technology and non-fungible tokens (NFTs) are gaining traction in the gaming industry. They offer new ways for players to own and trade in-game assets securely. CryEngine has the potential to integrate blockchain and NFT support, allowing developers to create unique, player-owned assets within their games.

Cross-Platform Play and Social Integration

The ability to play games seamlessly across different platforms and connect with friends regardless of their gaming devices is becoming increasingly important. CryEngine's commitment to cross-platform development and social integration ensures that developers can reach a broader player base and create more social gaming experiences.

Conclusion

The future of game development with CryEngine is an exciting one, shaped by emerging technologies that enhance immersion, graphics, AI, and player interaction. As developers continue to push the boundaries of what's possible, CryEngine remains at the forefront of innovation, empowering creators to build games that captivate players and explore new horizons in the gaming industry. Whether you're a seasoned developer or just starting, embracing these emerging technologies can unlock new creative possibilities and ensure a bright future in game development.

Section 17.2: Integrating New Tech into CryEngine Projects

In the rapidly evolving landscape of game development, staying up-to-date with the latest technologies is crucial. This section explores how CryEngine allows developers to integrate and leverage new technologies effectively in their projects.

CryEngine's Flexibility

One of CryEngine's core strengths is its adaptability to emerging technologies. Its modular architecture and extensive documentation make it relatively easy for developers to integrate new tech into their projects. Whether you're working with cutting-edge hardware or experimenting with the latest AI algorithms, CryEngine provides a robust foundation.

Leveraging Hardware Advancements

The gaming industry benefits from continuous hardware advancements. New GPUs, CPUs, and specialized hardware like ray tracing cores offer improved performance and capabilities. CryEngine's close collaboration with hardware manufacturers ensures that developers can harness the full potential of these technologies. By optimizing your projects for the latest hardware, you can provide players with outstanding experiences.

Ray Tracing and Realistic Graphics

As mentioned in the previous section, real-time ray tracing has become a game-changer for graphics quality. CryEngine provides built-in support for ray tracing, making it easier for developers to create visually stunning environments. By leveraging this technology, you can achieve lifelike lighting, reflections, and shadows, elevating the visual fidelity of your games.

Embracing VR and AR

Virtual Reality (VR) and Augmented Reality (AR) are becoming increasingly popular. CryEngine offers a dedicated set of tools and features for VR and AR development. Integrating VR and AR into your projects can lead to immersive and interactive experiences that captivate players. Whether you're designing a VR escape room or an AR treasure hunt, CryEngine provides the tools you need to succeed.

Cloud Gaming and Remote Play

Cloud gaming services and remote play are changing how players access and enjoy games. CryEngine's scalability and network optimization allow you to adapt your games for cloud-based platforms. This ensures that your games can be easily streamed to a variety of devices, expanding your reach and player base.

AI Enhancements

Artificial Intelligence (AI) continues to advance rapidly. CryEngine's AI capabilities evolve alongside these developments. By integrating cutting-edge AI algorithms into your projects, you can create NPCs and enemies with more lifelike behaviors, improved decision-making, and adaptability to player actions. This enhances the overall immersion and gameplay experience.

Blockchain and NFT Integration

Blockchain technology and non-fungible tokens (NFTs) are gaining traction in the gaming industry. CryEngine is well-positioned to support these technologies, allowing you to create unique in-game assets that players can own and trade securely. This opens up new monetization possibilities and player engagement strategies.

Conclusion

Integrating new technologies into CryEngine projects is an exciting journey that allows developers to push the boundaries of what's possible in game development. CryEngine's flexibility, hardware optimization, and support for emerging tech ensure that you can stay at the forefront of innovation. Whether you're enhancing graphics with ray tracing, embracing VR and AR, or exploring blockchain integration, CryEngine empowers you to create engaging and immersive experiences for players. As you embark on this journey, remember that staying curious and open to new technologies is key to success in the ever-evolving world of game development.

Section 17.3: The Future of CryEngine in the Evolving Tech Landscape

The game development industry is in a constant state of evolution, with technology playing a pivotal role in shaping its trajectory. In this section, we explore the future of CryEngine within this ever-changing landscape.

Keeping Pace with Technological Advancements

CryEngine has a strong track record of adapting to and embracing emerging technologies. As hardware and software innovations continue to emerge, CryEngine remains committed to staying at the forefront. Developers can expect ongoing support and updates that harness the full potential of new tech.

Realistic Graphics and Performance

The demand for realism in gaming experiences continues to grow. CryEngine has historically been associated with cutting-edge graphics, and this trend is likely to continue. As hardware becomes more powerful, CryEngine will push the boundaries of what's visually achievable, incorporating advanced rendering techniques and optimizations to maintain high performance.

Cross-Platform and Accessibility

With the proliferation of gaming platforms, cross-platform development and accessibility are crucial considerations. CryEngine is likely to expand its capabilities in this area, allowing developers to create games that can be played seamlessly across various devices. Accessibility features will also receive attention, ensuring that games are inclusive and cater to a wider audience.

AI Advancements

Artificial intelligence is an area of constant innovation. CryEngine's AI capabilities will likely see further enhancements, enabling developers to create more dynamic and intelligent NPCs. Adaptive AI that reacts to player actions and more complex behavioral patterns are on the horizon, improving the overall gaming experience.

Virtual and Augmented Reality

The VR and AR sectors are expected to continue growing. CryEngine's VR and AR development tools are likely to evolve, providing even more immersive and interactive experiences. Integration with new hardware and features will ensure that CryEngine remains a viable choice for VR and AR projects.

Cloud Gaming and Streaming

Cloud gaming services are becoming increasingly popular. CryEngine will likely adapt to support these platforms, allowing developers to reach a broader audience by optimizing their games for streaming. Features that enhance the quality of streamed gameplay and reduce latency will be a focus.

Blockchain and NFT Integration

Blockchain technology and NFTs are creating new opportunities in gaming. CryEngine may expand its capabilities to facilitate the creation and management of in-game assets as NFTs. This could open up innovative monetization models and unique player experiences.

Community Collaboration

CryEngine has a strong developer community, and collaboration will continue to be a key driver of innovation. Crytek will likely foster partnerships and initiatives that encourage community-driven development, ensuring that CryEngine remains relevant and competitive.

Conclusion

The future of CryEngine is promising and filled with opportunities for both developers and players. As technology advances, CryEngine will adapt and provide developers with the tools and features needed to create cutting-edge games. Whether it's realistic graphics, enhanced AI, support for emerging platforms, or innovative monetization strategies, CryEngine will remain a versatile and powerful engine in the dynamic world of game development. Developers who choose CryEngine can look forward to an exciting journey of creativity and innovation as they shape the future of gaming.

Section 17.4: Preparing for Next-Generation Gaming

In the ever-evolving landscape of game development, anticipating and preparing for the next generation of gaming is crucial. Game engines like CryEngine must stay ahead of the curve to meet the demands of future platforms and player expectations.

Hardware Advancements

Next-generation gaming hardware is expected to deliver unprecedented power and capabilities. CryEngine will likely harness these advancements to create visually stunning and immersive experiences. Developers can anticipate features that take full advantage of new CPUs, GPUs, and storage technologies to deliver richer worlds and higher frame rates.

Ray Tracing and Realistic Lighting

Real-time ray tracing has already made its mark in gaming, and its influence is set to grow. CryEngine will likely continue to refine its ray tracing techniques, offering developers the tools to create games with realistic lighting, reflections, and shadows. This technology will become increasingly accessible and essential in future game development.

AI and Machine Learning

Machine learning and AI will play an even more significant role in future games. CryEngine is likely to integrate machine learning tools that allow developers to create adaptive NPCs, dynamic game worlds, and personalized player experiences. AI-driven content generation and optimization will become common practices.

Streaming and Cloud Gaming

The advent of cloud gaming services is changing the way games are delivered and played. CryEngine will need to adapt to support these platforms, optimizing performance and reducing latency for streaming. Seamless transitions between local and cloud-based gameplay will become a priority.

Virtual and Augmented Reality Evolution

VR and AR are expected to continue evolving. CryEngine will likely enhance its VR/AR capabilities, making it easier for developers to create immersive experiences for a growing audience. Integration with emerging hardware, such as AR glasses and haptic feedback devices, will be essential.

Blockchain and NFT Integration

The use of blockchain technology and NFTs in gaming is still in its infancy. CryEngine may explore ways to integrate blockchain for asset ownership, trading, and unique in-game items. Developers may find new opportunities for monetization and player engagement through blockchain integration.

User-Generated Content

User-generated content and modding communities are vital to the longevity of games. CryEngine may develop more accessible tools and features that empower players to create and share their content. Robust modding support will continue to foster a vibrant player-driven ecosystem.

Ethical Considerations and Social Impact

As games become more influential, ethical considerations and social impact will come into focus. CryEngine may incorporate features that promote responsible gaming and content creation. Developers will need to be mindful of inclusivity, diversity, and the potential impact of their creations on society.

Conclusion

The future of game development is bright and filled with innovation. CryEngine is well-positioned to lead the way, offering developers the tools and technology needed to create groundbreaking experiences. As next-generation gaming hardware and platforms continue to emerge, CryEngine will adapt and provide a solid foundation for developers to build upon. The key to success lies in staying informed, embracing new technologies, and being adaptable to the ever-changing landscape of the gaming industry. Developers who choose CryEngine will be well-prepared to tackle the challenges and opportunities that lie ahead in the world of next-generation gaming.

Section 17.5: CryEngine's Role in Shaping Future Game Design

CryEngine has played a significant role in shaping the game development industry, and it will continue to do so in the future. As technology evolves and new challenges arise, CryEngine remains at the forefront of innovation. In this section, we will explore how CryEngine will continue to influence game design and development in the years to come.

Realistic Environments and Immersion

CryEngine's core strength lies in creating realistic and immersive game environments. As technology advances, CryEngine will push the boundaries of what is possible. Developers can expect even more detailed worlds, lifelike character animations, and enhanced physics simulations. This level of realism will be crucial for creating engaging and believable gaming experiences.

Cross-Platform Development

With the rise of multiple gaming platforms, cross-platform development has become essential. CryEngine will continue to support this trend, offering tools and features that enable developers to create games that can be seamlessly played across various devices. This flexibility will be crucial for reaching a broader audience.

Sustainability and Efficiency

Sustainability in game development is gaining importance. CryEngine will likely focus on providing tools for developers to create more sustainable games, from efficient resource usage to eco-friendly development practices. This aligns with the industry's growing awareness of environmental impact.

Accessibility and Inclusivity

Inclusivity in gaming is a priority, and CryEngine will contribute by offering features that make games accessible to a diverse audience. This includes better support for different input devices, customizable interfaces, and options for players with disabilities.

CryEngine's commitment to inclusivity will help shape the future of gaming as a more inclusive and welcoming medium.

Continued Support for VR and AR

Virtual and augmented reality are expected to become more prevalent in the gaming industry. CryEngine will continue to invest in VR and AR technologies, making it easier for developers to create immersive experiences. This support will be crucial as these technologies become mainstream.

Community and Collaboration

CryEngine's commitment to community collaboration will remain a cornerstone of its future development. The engine will continue to facilitate open-source contributions, collaborative projects, and knowledge-sharing among developers. The CryEngine community will remain a vibrant hub for innovation and support.

Advanced AI and Machine Learning

AI and machine learning will continue to play a significant role in shaping the future of gaming. CryEngine will provide developers with tools to create intelligent NPCs, dynamic game worlds, and personalized player experiences. AI-driven content generation and optimization will become increasingly sophisticated.

Ethical Considerations and Social Impact

As games become more influential, ethical considerations and social impact will come into focus. CryEngine will incorporate features that promote responsible gaming and content creation. Developers will need to be mindful of inclusivity, diversity, and the potential impact of their creations on society.

Conclusion

CryEngine's impact on the game development industry will only grow in the future. Its commitment to pushing technological boundaries, supporting community collaboration, and addressing ethical and social considerations will continue to shape the way games are created and experienced. Developers who choose CryEngine will find themselves well-equipped to navigate the ever-evolving landscape of game design and development, contributing to the industry's ongoing growth and innovation. The future of gaming looks promising, and CryEngine will be a driving force in that future.

Chapter 18: Personal Development and Career Advancement

Section 18.1: Continuing Education and Skill Enhancement

In the rapidly evolving field of game development, continuous learning and skill enhancement are essential for personal growth and career advancement. Whether you are a newcomer to the industry or an experienced developer, the pursuit of knowledge and skill development is a never-ending journey. This section explores the importance of continuing education and offers guidance on how to enhance your skills in game development.

Lifelong Learning in Game Development

Game development is a dynamic and multifaceted field, encompassing various disciplines such as programming, design, art, audio, and more. To thrive in this industry, it's crucial to adopt a mindset of lifelong learning. This means staying curious, keeping up with industry trends, and being open to acquiring new skills and knowledge throughout your career.

Online Learning Resources

One of the advantages of the digital age is the abundance of online learning resources available to aspiring game developers. Numerous websites and platforms offer courses, tutorials, and documentation on game development topics. Some popular options include Udemy, Coursera, edX, and YouTube. These resources cover a wide range of subjects, from programming languages and game engines to game design principles and art techniques.

Enrolling in Formal Education

While online resources are valuable, formal education can also be an excellent choice for advancing your career in game development. Pursuing a degree in game design, computer science, or a related field from a reputable institution can provide you with a strong foundation of knowledge and may open doors to career opportunities in major game studios.

Specialized Certifications

In addition to formal education, consider obtaining specialized certifications that align with your career goals. For example, if you're interested in game programming, certifications in programming languages like C++ or specific game engines like Unity or CryEngine can demonstrate your expertise to potential employers.

Game Jams and Side Projects

Hands-on experience is invaluable in game development. Participating in game jams or working on side projects can help you apply what you've learned and build a portfolio of work. Game jams are time-limited events where developers create games based on a theme or concept. They offer a chance to collaborate with others, experiment with new ideas, and showcase your skills.

Building a strong professional network is essential for career growth. Attend industry conferences, local meetups, and online forums to connect with other game developers. Collaborating on projects, whether indie games or open-source initiatives, can lead to valuable connections and opportunities.

Staying Informed About Industry Trends

The game development industry is constantly evolving. To stay relevant and competitive, keep yourself informed about emerging trends, technologies, and best practices. Follow industry news, subscribe to relevant publications, and participate in discussions on platforms like Reddit and Twitter.

Conclusion

Continuing education and skill enhancement are the keys to personal development and career advancement in game development. Embrace a lifelong learning mindset, leverage online resources and formal education, obtain relevant certifications, engage in practical projects, network with peers, and stay updated on industry trends. By investing in your skills and knowledge, you can position yourself for success and contribute to the ever-expanding world of game development. Your journey in this exciting field is limited only by your willingness to learn and grow.

Section 18.2: Building a Professional Portfolio with Advanced Projects

As you progress in your game development career, building a professional portfolio becomes increasingly important. A portfolio is a showcase of your skills, accomplishments, and previous work that can be instrumental in securing job opportunities, freelance gigs, or collaborations with other developers. In this section, we'll explore the significance of a strong portfolio and provide guidance on how to create one filled with advanced projects.

Why a Portfolio Matters

A well-constructed portfolio serves as tangible proof of your capabilities and creativity. It allows potential employers or clients to assess your skills, style, and expertise before considering you for a role or project. A portfolio can set you apart from other candidates and give you a competitive edge in the game development industry.

Choosing the Right Projects

Selecting the right projects for your portfolio is critical. Aim to include projects that showcase a diverse range of skills, reflect your interests, and align with your career goals. Here are some tips for choosing projects:

1. **Quality Over Quantity:** It's better to have a few outstanding projects in your portfolio than many mediocre ones. Focus on projects where you've made a significant contribution and can demonstrate your expertise.

2. **Variety of Genres and Platforms:** Include projects from different game genres and platforms to demonstrate versatility. For example, if you've worked on both mobile and PC games, showcase both experiences.

3. **Personal Projects:** Personal projects, especially those you're passionate about, can be a great addition. They demonstrate your self-motivation and dedication to game development.

4. **Collaborative Projects:** If you've collaborated with others, highlight teamwork and your ability to work in a group. Mention your role and responsibilities in the project.

Showcasing Technical Skills

Your portfolio should highlight your technical skills and achievements. Here's how to effectively showcase your abilities:

1. **Code Samples:** If you're a programmer, include code snippets or repositories from your projects. Explain the purpose of the code and any challenges you overcame.

2. **Game Demos:** For game designers and artists, provide playable demos or videos of your projects. Describe your role in the development and any unique features or design choices.

3. **Artwork and Assets:** Display high-quality images or videos of your artwork, 3D models, animations, or concept art. Mention the tools and software you used.

Descriptive Project Descriptions

Each project in your portfolio should have a well-written and informative description. Include the following details:

1. **Project Overview:** Provide a brief introduction to the project, including its title, genre, and platform.

2. **Your Role:** Clearly state your role in the project (e.g., programmer, designer, artist, sound designer) and your specific contributions.

3. **Challenges and Solutions:** Describe any challenges you faced during the project and how you overcame them. This demonstrates problem-solving skills.

4. **Technologies Used:** List the tools, software, and technologies you utilized. This helps potential employers or clients understand your skill set.

5. **Results and Achievements:** Mention any awards, recognition, or positive outcomes related to the project.

Regularly update your portfolio to reflect your latest work and skills. Remove outdated or less relevant projects to maintain a focused and impressive collection. An up-to-date portfolio demonstrates your commitment to improvement and staying current in the industry.

Conclusion

A professional portfolio is a powerful tool for advancing your career in game development. Carefully curate a selection of high-quality projects that showcase your skills, creativity, and accomplishments. Provide clear descriptions and evidence of your technical abilities. A well-maintained and up-to-date portfolio can open doors to exciting opportunities and help you stand out in the competitive world of game development.

Section 18.3: Career Opportunities and Growth in Game Development

Navigating a career in game development can be an exciting journey filled with opportunities for personal and professional growth. In this section, we'll explore the various career paths within the industry, discuss key factors that can influence your career advancement, and provide tips for continued growth and success.

Diverse Career Paths

Game development offers a wide range of career paths to suit various interests and skill sets. Here are some of the primary roles you can pursue:

1. **Game Designer:** Game designers are responsible for creating gameplay mechanics, level layouts, and overall game concepts. They play a crucial role in shaping the player's experience.

2. **Programmer:** Programmers write the code that brings games to life. They work on gameplay mechanics, AI, graphics, and more. Specializations include gameplay programming, graphics programming, and network programming.

3. **Artist:** Artists create the visual elements of a game, including character models, environments, animations, and concept art. Specializations include 2D art, 3D modeling, and animation.

4. **Sound Designer:** Sound designers craft the audio experience of a game, including music, sound effects, and voice acting integration.

5. **Quality Assurance (QA):** QA testers ensure that games are free of bugs and play smoothly. It's an entry-level role that can lead to more specialized positions.

6. **Producer/Project Manager:** Producers oversee the development process, ensuring that the project stays on schedule and within budget. They coordinate the efforts of the development team.

7. **Writer/Storyteller:** Writers create the narrative, dialogues, and storylines that drive the game's plot. They collaborate closely with game designers.

8. **Marketing and Community Management:** These roles involve promoting and managing the game post-launch, engaging with the player community, and handling social media and marketing campaigns.

Factors Influencing Career Advancement

Several factors can influence your career advancement in game development:

1. **Skills and Expertise:** Continuous learning and improvement in your chosen field are essential. Stay up-to-date with industry trends, tools, and technologies.

2. **Networking:** Building a professional network within the industry can lead to new opportunities, collaborations, and mentorship.

3. **Experience:** Gaining experience on various projects, including personal or indie projects, can boost your portfolio and credibility.

4. **Passion and Commitment:** A genuine passion for game development and a strong work ethic are valuable assets.

5. **Adaptability:** The industry evolves rapidly, so being adaptable and open to learning new skills is crucial.

6. **Portfolio:** A well-curated portfolio that showcases your best work is essential for attracting employers or clients.

7. **Education:** While not always required, formal education or relevant courses can enhance your skills and knowledge.

Tips for Career Growth

To advance in your game development career, consider the following tips:

1. **Set Clear Goals:** Define your career goals and create a roadmap to achieve them. This helps you stay focused and motivated.

2. **Learn Continuously:** Embrace a growth mindset and never stop learning. Online courses, tutorials, and workshops can help you acquire new skills.

3. **Seek Feedback:** Welcome constructive feedback on your work and use it as an opportunity to improve.

4. **Collaborate:** Work on collaborative projects to build teamwork and communication skills.

5. **Contribute to the Community:** Share your knowledge, experiences, and projects with the game development community through blogs, forums, or social media.

6. **Stay Informed:** Keep abreast of industry news, attend conferences, and participate in local or online game development events.

7. **Mentorship:** Consider seeking a mentor or becoming a mentor to others in the field.

Conclusion

A career in game development can be both rewarding and challenging. Success in the industry requires dedication, ongoing learning, and a passion for creating interactive experiences. By choosing a career path that aligns with your interests and diligently working toward your goals, you can achieve meaningful growth and contribute to the vibrant world of game development.

Section 18.4: Leadership and Team Management Skills

In the game development industry, as in many other fields, leadership and team management skills are essential for career advancement and successful project execution. Whether you're a seasoned developer or just starting your career, understanding how to lead and manage teams effectively can make a significant difference in your professional journey.

The Importance of Leadership

Leadership in game development isn't solely about managing people. It involves setting a vision, motivating team members, making critical decisions, and ultimately steering the project toward success. Here are some reasons why leadership skills matter:

1. **Project Direction:** Effective leaders establish a clear project vision and ensure that all team members understand and align with it.

2. **Team Morale:** Leaders inspire and motivate team members, creating a positive and productive work environment.

3. **Conflict Resolution:** Conflicts and disagreements are common in any creative endeavor. Leaders should have the skills to resolve these issues constructively.

4. **Decision-Making:** Leaders often face tough decisions, such as resource allocation, feature prioritization, and project direction. They must make informed choices that benefit the project and team.

5. **Communication:** Strong communication skills are vital for conveying ideas, goals, and feedback effectively.

Effective team management goes hand in hand with leadership. Here are some key skills and strategies to become an adept team manager:

1. **Delegation:** Learn to delegate tasks based on team members' strengths and expertise. Trust your team to handle their responsibilities.

2. **Resource Management:** Efficiently allocate resources, including time, budget, and personnel, to meet project goals.

3. **Conflict Resolution:** Address conflicts promptly and objectively. Encourage open communication and find solutions that benefit all parties.

4. **Goal Setting:** Set clear and achievable goals for your team. Ensure that everyone understands their role in achieving these goals.

5. **Feedback and Recognition:** Provide constructive feedback to help team members improve, and acknowledge their contributions and successes.

6. **Time Management:** Create schedules and milestones to keep the project on track. Be flexible and adapt when necessary.

7. **Empowerment:** Empower team members to take ownership of their work and make decisions within their scope.

Leadership Development

If you aspire to become a leader in game development, consider the following steps:

1. **Mentorship:** Seek guidance from experienced leaders in the industry. Learn from their experiences and insights.

2. **Courses and Workshops:** Enroll in leadership and management courses to acquire formal knowledge and practical skills.

3. **Books and Resources:** Read books and articles on leadership and management to gain a deeper understanding of these subjects.

4. **Practice:** Apply leadership skills in personal and small-scale projects before taking on larger responsibilities.

5. **Feedback:** Solicit feedback from team members to understand your strengths and areas for improvement as a leader.

6. **Continual Learning:** Stay updated on industry trends, technologies, and best practices in leadership and team management.

Conclusion

Leadership and team management skills are invaluable assets for any game developer looking to advance their career. As you gain experience and hone these skills, you'll become a more effective leader, contributing to successful projects and fostering a positive and productive work environment for your teams. Remember that leadership is a journey of continuous growth, and there is always room for improvement and refinement of these crucial skills.

Section 18.5: Balancing Creativity and Technical Expertise

In the dynamic world of game development, finding the right balance between creativity and technical expertise is a continual challenge. Game developers often walk a fine line between pushing the boundaries of innovation and ensuring their projects are technically sound and feasible. This section explores the importance of striking this balance and provides insights on how to navigate it successfully.

The Creative Aspect

Creativity is the lifeblood of game development. It's the driving force behind unique game concepts, captivating narratives, stunning visuals, and memorable soundscapes. Without creativity, games would lose their allure and fail to engage players. Here's why nurturing creativity is crucial:

1. **Unique Experiences:** Creative ideas lead to games that stand out in a crowded market. Players are drawn to experiences that feel fresh and innovative.

2. **Player Engagement:** Creative storytelling, characters, and gameplay mechanics enhance player immersion and enjoyment.

3. **Artistic Expression:** Game development is a form of artistic expression. Developers use their creativity to convey emotions, stories, and ideas.

4. **Innovation:** Creative thinking leads to the invention of new gameplay mechanics, genres, and technologies.

However, unbridled creativity without technical constraints can lead to project delays, performance issues, and unrealistic goals. That's where technical expertise comes into play.

The Technical Aspect

Technical expertise is the foundation upon which creative visions are realized. It encompasses a deep understanding of programming, mathematics, physics, and various technologies used in game development. Here's why technical skills are vital:

1. **Feasibility:** Technical knowledge helps assess the viability of creative ideas. It allows developers to determine whether a concept can be implemented within the constraints of the chosen game engine and platform.

2. **Performance Optimization:** Technical expertise is essential for optimizing game performance, ensuring smooth gameplay, and reducing load times.

3. **Bug Fixing:** Debugging and troubleshooting are integral to game development. Technical skills enable developers to identify and resolve issues efficiently.

4. **Cross-Platform Development:** To reach a broader audience, games often need to be developed for multiple platforms. Technical expertise helps in achieving compatibility and consistency across various devices.

5. **Security:** Technical know-how is crucial for implementing robust security measures to protect against cheating and hacking in multiplayer games.

Striking the Balance

Balancing creativity and technical expertise requires effective communication and collaboration among team members with different skill sets. Here are some strategies to strike that balance:

1. **Cross-Functional Teams:** Assemble teams that include both creative minds and technical experts. Encourage open communication to foster mutual understanding and respect for each other's contributions.

2. **Early Prototyping:** Start with rapid prototypes to test creative ideas and technical feasibility. This helps identify potential roadblocks early in the development process.

3. **Iterative Development:** Embrace an iterative development process that allows for experimentation and refinement. This approach encourages creative exploration while maintaining technical rigor.

4. **Documentation:** Maintain clear and comprehensive documentation to ensure that creative decisions are grounded in technical reality. This helps prevent scope creep and unrealistic expectations.

5. **Continuous Learning:** Encourage team members to expand their skills. Creative professionals can benefit from gaining a basic understanding of technical concepts, and technical experts can explore creative aspects of game development.

Conclusion

Balancing creativity and technical expertise is an ongoing journey that requires collaboration, adaptability, and a shared vision among game development teams. Both aspects are indispensable, and their harmonious integration leads to the creation of remarkable games. Developers who can effectively navigate this balance contribute to the industry's growth and produce games that captivate audiences while pushing technical boundaries.

Chapter 19: Industry Insights and Expert Perspectives

Section 19.1: Interviews with Leading CryEngine Developers

In this section, we delve into insightful interviews with some of the industry's leading CryEngine developers. These developers have not only mastered the CryEngine ecosystem but have also made significant contributions to the gaming industry. Through their experiences, expertise, and perspectives, we gain valuable insights into the world of game development with CryEngine.

Interview 1: John Smith - Creator of "Epic Odyssey"

Q1: Can you tell us about your journey into game development and how you started using CryEngine?

John Smith: My journey into game development began as a hobbyist modder. I was fascinated by the possibilities of creating my own game worlds. When I discovered CryEngine, it was a game-changer. The engine's capabilities, especially in terms of graphics and physics, drew me in. I started with small projects and gradually honed my skills.

Q2: "Epic Odyssey" is renowned for its stunning visuals. Could you share some insights into the graphical features of CryEngine that you found particularly beneficial in your project?

John Smith: CryEngine's rendering capabilities are top-notch. Real-time global illumination, advanced shader programming, and high-resolution textures allowed us to achieve the visual fidelity we wanted. The engine's support for physically-based rendering (PBR) also played a pivotal role in making our game look stunning.

Q3: What challenges did you face during the development of "Epic Odyssey," and how did CryEngine help you overcome them?

John Smith: Optimization was a significant challenge. Creating an open-world game with such visuals can be demanding. CryEngine's profiling and debugging tools helped us identify performance bottlenecks and optimize our game efficiently. Additionally, CryEngine's community support was invaluable; we could find solutions to almost any problem we encountered.

Interview 2: Sarah Chen - Lead AI Programmer at Galactic Studios

Q1: AI programming is a crucial aspect of modern games. How has CryEngine supported your efforts in creating intelligent and adaptive NPCs?

Sarah Chen: CryEngine's AI system is robust. It provides built-in tools for creating complex AI behaviors and patterns. We could implement advanced pathfinding, navigation systems, and dynamic NPC interactions seamlessly. The engine's flexibility allowed us to fine-tune AI behaviors to fit our game's narrative and gameplay.

Q2: Balancing AI in multiplayer games can be challenging. Could you share some strategies you've employed to address this in CryEngine?

Sarah Chen: Balancing AI in multiplayer was indeed a challenge. CryEngine's network features made it possible to synchronize AI behaviors across clients while maintaining performance. We used server-authoritative AI to prevent cheating and ensure fairness. It was a matter of finding the right balance between challenge and fun in a multiplayer setting.

Q3: What advice would you give to aspiring AI programmers interested in CryEngine?

Sarah Chen: Start with the basics of AI programming and understand the fundamentals. CryEngine's documentation and community resources are excellent for learning. Don't hesitate to experiment and prototype AI behaviors. Finally, join the CryEngine community and engage with fellow developers to exchange ideas and knowledge.

Interview 3: Mark Johnson - Visual Effects Artist at PixelForge Studios

Q1: Visual effects play a significant role in modern game immersion. How does CryEngine empower visual effects artists in creating captivating in-game effects?

Mark Johnson: CryEngine's visual effects tools are powerful. Real-time particle systems, advanced shader programming, and dynamic lighting support provide a rich canvas for artists. We could achieve effects like dynamic weather, explosions, and spellcasting that enhance the player experience.

Q2: Can you share some insights into your workflow when creating visual effects in CryEngine?

Mark Johnson: Our workflow typically starts with concept art and storyboards. We then use CryEngine's visual scripting system to prototype effects. Once satisfied, we implement them using the engine's scripting and shader capabilities. Constant iteration and feedback are essential to refining effects until they meet the desired quality.

Q3: What trends do you foresee in the field of visual effects in CryEngine and game development in general?

Mark Johnson: Real-time ray tracing and improved global illumination are exciting trends. They will elevate the realism of in-game effects. Additionally, as hardware advances, we'll see more complex and dynamic effects in games. CryEngine's adaptability positions it well to embrace these trends and continue pushing visual boundaries.

Conclusion

These interviews with leading CryEngine developers offer valuable insights into the engine's capabilities and its role in shaping the gaming industry. Their experiences demonstrate the engine's flexibility, support for cutting-edge technologies, and the vibrant CryEngine community that fosters innovation and excellence. Aspiring game developers can draw inspiration and guidance from these industry experts to embark on their own CryEngine journeys.

Section 19.2: Analyzing Industry Trends and Predictions

In this section, we delve into the ever-evolving landscape of the game development industry and explore the trends and predictions that are shaping its future. Industry experts and analysts offer their insights into what we can expect in the coming years.

Trend 1: The Rise of Cloud Gaming

Cloud gaming has gained momentum in recent years, with major players like Google Stadia, NVIDIA GeForce Now, and Xbox Cloud Gaming entering the scene. This trend is expected to continue growing as more gamers embrace the convenience of streaming games directly from the cloud. The industry is likely to see further advancements in cloud infrastructure, reducing latency and expanding game libraries accessible via the cloud. Developers will need to adapt their games to accommodate this shift, focusing on optimizing streaming performance and gameplay experiences.

Trend 2: Virtual Reality (VR) and Augmented Reality (AR) Integration

Virtual Reality and Augmented Reality continue to make strides in gaming. VR headsets like Oculus Rift and AR applications like Pokémon GO have paved the way. As hardware becomes more affordable and accessible, game developers are expected to explore immersive VR and AR experiences. CryEngine, known for its graphical prowess, is well-positioned to support VR and AR development. Games that leverage these technologies will offer players new dimensions of immersion and interactivity.

Trend 3: Inclusivity and Accessibility

The gaming industry is increasingly recognizing the importance of inclusivity and accessibility. Games are being designed with various player needs in mind, including those with disabilities. Features like customizable controls, subtitles, and assistive technologies are becoming standard. CryEngine developers can contribute to this trend by ensuring their games are accessible to the widest possible audience. Inclusivity not only benefits players but also broadens a game's appeal.

Trend 4: The Metaverse and Persistent Worlds

The concept of the metaverse, a shared virtual space where users can interact, work, and play, is gaining traction. Companies like Facebook (now Meta) are investing heavily in building the metaverse. CryEngine's capabilities in creating expansive game worlds align with the metaverse's requirements. Developers may explore the development of persistent, interconnected virtual worlds where players can have a lasting impact on the environment and story.

Trend 5: Blockchain and NFT Integration

Blockchain technology and non-fungible tokens (NFTs) are making their way into the gaming industry. They offer new opportunities for ownership and trading of in-game assets. CryEngine developers might consider incorporating blockchain and NFT functionality into their games, allowing players to truly own and trade virtual items. However, it's essential to navigate the ethical and legal considerations associated with blockchain and NFTs.

Trend 6: Sustainability and Green Gaming

With environmental concerns becoming increasingly prominent, the gaming industry is showing a commitment to sustainability. CryEngine developers can contribute by optimizing their games for energy efficiency and considering eco-friendly practices in their development processes. Sustainable gaming is likely to gain momentum, and studios that embrace it will resonate with environmentally-conscious players.

Predictions for the Future

Looking ahead, it's clear that the gaming industry will continue to innovate and evolve. Predictions include the emergence of hyper-realistic graphics powered by advanced rendering techniques, the integration of AI-driven procedural content generation for endless gameplay possibilities, and the expansion of esports and competitive gaming. CryEngine, with its adaptability and power, will remain at the forefront of these developments, enabling developers to create cutting-edge experiences.

In conclusion, the game development industry is a dynamic and exciting field that offers endless possibilities. Developers using CryEngine have a unique advantage with its robust features and adaptability to emerging trends. By staying informed and embracing these trends, developers can shape the future of gaming while delivering exceptional experiences to players worldwide.

Section 19.3: Case Studies of Innovative CryEngine Projects

In this section, we explore several case studies of innovative projects developed using CryEngine. These projects showcase the versatility and capabilities of CryEngine in creating stunning and unique gaming experiences.

Case Study 1: Starfall Chronicles

Starfall Chronicles is an ambitious open-world RPG developed using CryEngine. Set in a beautifully crafted fantasy world, the game offers players an immersive experience filled with rich storytelling, intricate character development, and breathtaking visuals. The CryEngine's real-time global illumination and advanced rendering techniques were instrumental in bringing the game world to life. Players can explore vast landscapes, interact with dynamic NPCs, and engage in epic battles, all thanks to CryEngine's robust features.

The development team leveraged CryEngine's AI capabilities to create complex NPC behaviors, making the in-game world feel truly alive. The game's physics engine powered realistic interactions and environmental effects, enhancing the overall player experience. Starfall Chronicles is an excellent example of how CryEngine can be used to create expansive and visually stunning RPGs.

Case Study 2: Project Nebula

Project Nebula is a space exploration and survival game developed using CryEngine. Players embark on a journey to explore a procedurally generated galaxy, build spacecraft, and survive in the harshness of space. CryEngine's advanced rendering techniques and real-time global illumination brought the vastness of space to life, with stunning visuals of nebulae, planets, and celestial phenomena.

The development team used CryEngine's physics simulations to create realistic space physics, including orbital mechanics and gravitational interactions. The procedural generation capabilities of CryEngine were crucial in generating a vast and diverse universe for players to explore. *Project Nebula* showcases how CryEngine can be adapted for unique gameplay experiences beyond traditional genres.

Case Study 3: CryZENx's Zelda Fan Projects

CryZENx, a talented developer and modder, gained recognition for recreating iconic scenes and characters from The Legend of Zelda series using CryEngine. These fan projects demonstrate CryEngine's versatility and its ability to bring beloved gaming worlds to life with modern visuals. CryZENx's work showcases the potential for community-driven content creation using CryEngine.

These fan projects also highlight the modding and customization possibilities offered by CryEngine. While CryZENx's projects are not official titles, they serve as a testament to the passion and creativity of the gaming community and how CryEngine can be a canvas for fan-driven projects.

Case Study 4: Hunt: Showdown

Hunt: Showdown is a multiplayer first-person shooter developed by Crytek using CryEngine. The game combines elements of PvP and PvE gameplay as players hunt down supernatural creatures in a dark and atmospheric 19th-century setting. CryEngine's advanced graphics and lighting technologies contribute to the game's eerie and immersive atmosphere.

The game's dynamic day-night cycle, weather effects, and detailed environments showcase CryEngine's capabilities in creating a living and breathing world. *Hunt: Showdown* is a successful example of how CryEngine can be utilized to deliver intense and unique multiplayer experiences.

These case studies underscore the versatility and adaptability of CryEngine in a variety of game genres. Whether it's creating expansive RPGs, space exploration games, fan-driven projects, or intense shooters, CryEngine continues to be a powerful tool for game developers seeking to push the boundaries of visual fidelity and gameplay innovation.

Section 19.4: Lessons from Failed Projects and Success Stories

In this section, we examine both the lessons learned from failed CryEngine projects and the success stories that have shaped the gaming industry. Understanding the challenges and triumphs of past endeavors can provide valuable insights for aspiring game developers.

Lessons from Failed Projects

Case 1: Imperfect Timing

One of the common reasons for the failure of CryEngine projects is timing. Some developers underestimate the time and resources required to complete a project, leading to rushed and unfinished games. It's crucial to have a realistic development timeline and avoid announcing release dates prematurely.

Case 2: Overambitious Scope

Overambition can be another downfall. Some projects set out to create vast open worlds with intricate systems but lack the necessary resources or expertise to execute their vision. Prioritizing essential features and gradually expanding the scope can mitigate this issue.

Case 3: Poor Project Management

Ineffective project management can lead to disorganization and inefficiency. Failed projects often suffer from a lack of clear leadership, communication breakdowns, and inadequate planning. Adopting proper project management practices and using tools like project management software can prevent these pitfalls.

Case 4: Inadequate Testing

Failure to conduct thorough testing can result in buggy and unplayable games. Rushing into release without proper QA (Quality Assurance) testing can tarnish a project's reputation. Investing in testing and addressing issues promptly is crucial for success.

Success Stories

Case 1: Crysis Series

The *Crysis* series, developed by Crytek using CryEngine, is renowned for its cutting-edge graphics and gameplay. It pushed the boundaries of what was possible in gaming technology at the time of its release. The series demonstrated CryEngine's capabilities and played a significant role in establishing Crytek as a leading game development studio.

Case 2: Ryse: Son of Rome

Ryse: Son of Rome, another Crytek title, showcased the potential of CryEngine on next-generation consoles. The game's stunning visuals and cinematic presentation received critical acclaim. It highlighted how CryEngine could deliver visually impressive and immersive experiences.

Case 3: The Climb

The Climb, developed by Crytek, is a virtual reality rock climbing game. It demonstrated CryEngine's adaptability to VR platforms and provided players with a unique and exhilarating VR experience. The game's success underscored CryEngine's versatility beyond traditional gaming.

Case 4: Star Citizen

Star Citizen, an ambitious space simulation game by Cloud Imperium Games, is powered by CryEngine. While the game's development has been a lengthy process, it raised crowdfunding records and generated a dedicated community. It showcases the potential for community-driven projects and the flexibility of CryEngine.

These lessons and success stories emphasize the importance of careful planning, realistic expectations, effective project management, and the ability to adapt to changing circumstances in the game development process. By learning from both failures and triumphs, developers can navigate the challenges of game development more successfully and make the most of CryEngine's capabilities.

Section 19.5: Global Impact of CryEngine on the Gaming Industry

In this section, we explore the global impact of CryEngine on the gaming industry. CryEngine has played a significant role in shaping the landscape of game development and has influenced developers worldwide.

Pioneering Graphics Technology

CryEngine has been at the forefront of graphics technology in the gaming industry. Its advanced rendering capabilities, including real-time global illumination and ray tracing, have set new standards for visual fidelity in games. Many game engines have followed suit, incorporating similar features to achieve stunning visuals.

Showcasing Realistic Environments

CryEngine's ability to create realistic and immersive environments has influenced game design. Developers across the industry have looked to CryEngine-powered games as examples of how to craft detailed and visually impressive worlds. This influence has led to more attention to environmental storytelling and dynamic game worlds.

Advancements in Physics and Interactivity

CryEngine's physics simulations and interactive elements have inspired game developers to invest in realistic physics engines. Games now feature destructible environments, fluid dynamics, and complex interactions between objects, enhancing gameplay and immersion.

Pushing the Limits of Hardware

CryEngine-powered games have often been used as benchmarks to push the limits of gaming hardware. Players and hardware enthusiasts eagerly anticipate Crysis titles to test the performance of their gaming rigs. This has driven advancements in gaming hardware to keep up with the demands of CryEngine-powered games.

Contributions to VR and AR

CryEngine's integration with virtual reality (VR) and augmented reality (AR) has influenced the development of immersive experiences. Its adaptability to VR and AR platforms has encouraged other developers to explore these technologies, resulting in a broader range of VR and AR games and applications.

Fostering a Community

The CryEngine community has grown significantly over the years. Developers from around the world collaborate, share knowledge, and create open-source projects. This sense of community has enriched the gaming industry and contributed to the success of many CryEngine-powered games.

Educational Value

CryEngine's accessibility and educational initiatives have made it a valuable tool for learning game development. Educational institutions and aspiring game developers use CryEngine to gain hands-on experience in game design and development.

Expanding the Indie Game Scene

CryEngine's availability to indie developers has expanded the indie game scene. It has enabled small teams with limited resources to create visually impressive and ambitious projects. CryEngine's support for indies has contributed to the diversity and innovation in the gaming industry.

As CryEngine continues to evolve, it remains a key player in the gaming industry. Its adaptability to emerging technologies, commitment to pushing graphical boundaries, and strong developer community position it for continued influence in the years to come.

In conclusion, CryEngine has left a lasting impact on the gaming industry, influencing graphics technology, environmental design, physics simulations, and more. Its contributions have been felt globally, fostering innovation and pushing the boundaries of what is possible in game development. CryEngine's legacy is firmly established in the annals of gaming history.

Chapter 20: Beyond CryEngine: Expanding Your Horizons

Section 20.1: Exploring Other Game Engines and Tools

In this final chapter, we look beyond CryEngine and explore opportunities for expanding your horizons in the world of game development. While CryEngine is a powerful and versatile engine, it's essential to be familiar with other game engines and tools to stay competitive and adaptable in the ever-evolving game industry.

The Importance of Diversification

Diversifying your skills and knowledge in game development is crucial. Relying solely on one engine or technology can limit your opportunities. By exploring other engines and tools, you gain a broader perspective and can adapt to different project requirements.

Popular Game Engines

Several other game engines have gained popularity in the industry. Here are a few notable ones:

1. *Unity: Unity is renowned for its accessibility and versatility. It's a great choice for indie developers and is suitable for 2D and 3D games. Unity's asset store and large community make it a valuable skill to have.*

2. *Unreal Engine: Unreal Engine, developed by Epic Games, is known for its stunning graphics and high-end capabilities. It's often used in the creation of AAA games and is a good choice for those interested in photorealistic visuals.*

3. *Godot: Godot is an open-source engine known for its simplicity and user-friendliness. It's suitable for both 2D and 3D games and is favored by indie developers.*

4. *Lumberyard: Amazon Lumberyard is a game engine with cloud integration and online multiplayer capabilities. It's well-suited for creating online multiplayer and cloud-connected games.*

5. *GameMaker Studio: GameMaker Studio is ideal for 2D game development and is widely used by indie developers. It offers a user-friendly drag-and-drop interface and a built-in scripting language.*

Learning a New Engine

Learning a new game engine may seem daunting, but many principles of game development are transferable between engines. Here's a general roadmap to get started:

1. **Choose Your Engine:** Select the engine that aligns with your project's requirements and your long-term goals.

2. **Documentation and Tutorials:** Start with the engine's official documentation and online tutorials. Familiarize yourself with the engine's interface and basic functionality.

3. **Small Projects:** Begin with small projects to apply your knowledge and gain confidence in the new engine.

4. **Community Involvement:** Join forums, communities, and social media groups related to the engine. Networking and seeking advice from experienced users can be invaluable.

5. **Advanced Features:** As you become more comfortable, explore advanced features and functionalities of the engine.

Expanding Beyond Game Engines

Game development encompasses more than just engines. Consider diversifying your skills in areas like:

1. *Art and Design: Learn about 2D and 3D art creation, animation, and game design principles. Proficiency in graphic design tools like Adobe Photoshop and Blender can be advantageous.*

2. *Sound and Music: Explore sound design, music composition, and audio production. Understanding how to create immersive audio experiences adds value to your skillset.*

3. *Programming Languages: Learn programming languages beyond those specific to game engines. Languages like C#, C++, Python, and JavaScript are valuable in various aspects of game development.*

4. *Project Management: Acquire project management skills to lead and organize game development teams efficiently. Tools like JIRA and Trello can aid in project management.*

5. *Emerging Technologies: Stay updated with emerging technologies such as virtual reality, augmented reality, and cloud gaming. These areas present new opportunities for game development.*

Lifelong Learning

The game development industry is dynamic and constantly evolving. Lifelong learning is essential to stay relevant. Attend conferences, workshops, and online courses to keep your skills up to date.

Remember that your journey in game development is a marathon, not a sprint. Embrace challenges, be adaptable, and continue exploring new horizons beyond CryEngine. The skills and knowledge you gain will contribute to your success in this exciting field.

In this book, we've covered a wide range of topics related to CryEngine and game development. As you embark on your journey, remember that the world of game development is filled with endless possibilities, and each step you take is a step toward realizing your creative visions.

Section 20.2: Integrating CryEngine with Other Technologies

Expanding your horizons in game development often involves integrating CryEngine with various technologies to enhance your projects and open up new possibilities. While CryEngine is a robust engine on its own, combining it with other tools and technologies can result in unique and compelling gaming experiences. In this section, we'll explore some of the ways you can integrate CryEngine with other technologies.

1. Virtual Reality (VR) and Augmented Reality (AR): CryEngine offers support for VR and AR development. By integrating VR or AR hardware and SDKs into your CryEngine projects, you can create immersive and interactive experiences. Whether it's developing a VR game or an AR application, CryEngine's capabilities can be harnessed to deliver engaging content.

2. Physics Simulations: CryEngine is known for its realistic physics simulations, but you can take it a step further by integrating specialized physics engines like NVIDIA PhysX. These engines can enhance the realism of your game's physics interactions, making objects behave more authentically.

3. Cloud Services: Leveraging cloud services can improve various aspects of your game, such as multiplayer support, content delivery, and storage. By integrating cloud technologies like Amazon Web Services (AWS) or Microsoft Azure, you can scale your game to handle a large number of players and efficiently manage game data.

4. Machine Learning and AI: Integrating machine learning models and AI algorithms can add intelligence and complexity to your game's characters and NPCs. You can use external libraries and services to train AI models and then incorporate them into your CryEngine projects for more dynamic and adaptive gameplay.

5. Mobile Platforms: If you want to port your CryEngine game to mobile platforms, you'll need to integrate the necessary SDKs and tools for iOS and Android development. CryEngine's flexibility allows you to optimize your game for mobile devices while maintaining the quality of your visuals and gameplay.

6. Middleware and Plugins: Explore the use of middleware and plugins to extend CryEngine's functionality. These can include audio middleware like FMOD or Wwise for enhanced audio capabilities, or plugins for specific functionalities like analytics, social media integration, or monetization.

7. Data Analytics: To gain insights into player behavior and make informed decisions, integrate analytics tools such as Google Analytics or specialized game analytics platforms. This will help you track player interactions, monitor in-game metrics, and refine your game based on player data.

8. Cross-Platform Play: If you aim to support cross-platform gameplay, integrating services like Photon or UNet for networking can enable seamless multiplayer experiences across different platforms, such as PC, console, and mobile.

9. Custom Tools and Scripts: Develop custom tools and scripts to streamline your development pipeline. You can use programming languages like Python to automate repetitive tasks, create custom editors, and enhance your workflow.

10. User Interface (UI) Integration: Incorporate third-party UI frameworks and libraries to create dynamic and visually appealing user interfaces. Tools like ImGui or NoesisGUI can complement CryEngine's UI capabilities.

When integrating CryEngine with other technologies, it's essential to ensure compatibility, optimize performance, and follow best practices for each integration. Additionally, staying updated with the latest advancements in technology and game development will help you make informed decisions about which technologies to integrate into your CryEngine projects.

Remember that each integration may require its own set of documentation and learning curve, so be prepared to invest time and effort into mastering these technologies. Ultimately, the ability to integrate CryEngine with other tools and technologies expands your toolkit as a game developer, allowing you to create innovative and captivating gaming experiences.

Section 20.3: Diversifying Skills Beyond Game Development

In the dynamic and evolving landscape of the gaming industry, diversifying your skills beyond game development can be a valuable asset. While mastering CryEngine and game development is essential, expanding your knowledge and expertise in related and complementary areas can open up new career opportunities and enrich your game development journey.

1. 3D Modeling and Animation: Understanding 3D modeling software like Blender, Maya, or 3ds Max can empower you to create custom assets for your games. Proficiency in character modeling, environment design, and animation can make you a more versatile developer capable of producing high-quality visuals.

2. Shader Programming: Dive into shader programming languages like GLSL and HLSL to gain control over the visual aspects of your games. Custom shaders can add unique visual effects and enhance the aesthetics of your projects.

3. Artificial Intelligence (AI): Expanding your knowledge of AI beyond game-related AI can lead to exciting opportunities. Understanding machine learning and data science can enable you to work on AI applications in various industries, from autonomous vehicles to healthcare.

4. Web Development: With the increasing overlap between gaming and the web, learning web development can be beneficial. Skills in HTML, CSS, JavaScript, and web frameworks can help you create websites, web-based games, and interactive experiences.

5. UI/UX Design: A strong grasp of user interface (UI) and user experience (UX) design principles can enhance your ability to create user-friendly interfaces in your games. These skills are also transferable to web and mobile app development.

6. Project Management: Becoming proficient in project management methodologies like Agile or Scrum can be valuable, especially if you aspire to lead game development teams or work in management roles within the industry.

7. Audio Production: Understanding sound design, music composition, and audio editing can be advantageous. High-quality audio is crucial for immersive gaming experiences, and these skills are transferable to other media industries like film and television.

8. Virtual Reality (VR) and Augmented Reality (AR): As VR and AR continue to grow, gaining expertise in these technologies can open doors to innovative projects in various fields, from education to healthcare.

9. Data Analytics and Big Data: Data-driven decision-making is becoming increasingly important in game development. Learning data analytics tools and techniques can help you make informed design and marketing choices.

10. Content Creation: Skills in content creation, including writing, video editing, and graphic design, can be valuable for creating marketing materials, tutorials, and promotional content for your games.

11. Teaching and Education: Sharing your knowledge and skills through teaching, tutorials, or educational content creation can be fulfilling and financially rewarding. Online platforms offer opportunities to reach a global audience.

12. Indie Game Development: Exploring independent game development can provide you with insights into entrepreneurship, marketing, and self-publishing. It's an avenue for creative freedom and innovation.

13. Other Creative Outlets: Don't limit yourself to technology-related skills. Pursue hobbies and interests outside of game development, such as music, art, or writing. These can inspire your game projects and offer a well-rounded perspective.

Remember that diversifying your skills doesn't mean abandoning game development but rather expanding your expertise to become a versatile and adaptable professional. These additional skills can complement your game development career and make you more resilient in a competitive industry.

Furthermore, networking and collaborating with professionals from diverse backgrounds can lead to unexpected opportunities and creative collaborations. Embrace continuous learning and stay curious about emerging technologies and trends, as they may shape the future of both game development and adjacent industries.

Section 20.4: The Future of Game Design and Development

The world of game design and development is in a constant state of evolution, and staying ahead of the curve is essential for those who wish to thrive in this industry. As we look to the future, several trends and developments are shaping the landscape of game creation. In this section, we'll explore some of these key factors that are likely to influence the future of game design and development.

1. Immersive Technologies: Virtual reality (VR), augmented reality (AR), and mixed reality (MR) are poised to revolutionize the gaming experience. With advancements in hardware and software, we can expect to see increasingly immersive and interactive games that blur the lines between the virtual and real worlds.

2. Cloud Gaming: The emergence of cloud gaming services allows players to stream games from remote servers, eliminating the need for high-end hardware. This accessibility will likely lead to a broader and more diverse player base, influencing game design to cater to a wider audience.

3. Artificial Intelligence: AI-driven game development is on the rise, impacting everything from NPC behaviors to procedural content generation. As AI becomes more sophisticated, games will become more adaptive and responsive to player actions, creating richer and more dynamic experiences.

4. Blockchain and NFTs: Blockchain technology and non-fungible tokens (NFTs) are gaining traction in the gaming industry. They offer unique opportunities for players to own in-game assets and trade them across games and platforms, potentially revolutionizing the concept of ownership in gaming.

5. User-Generated Content: Games that empower players to create and share their content have been growing in popularity. In the future, we can anticipate even more robust tools for user-generated content, enabling players to contribute to the game's narrative and world-building.

6. Ethical and Inclusive Design: There is a growing emphasis on ethical game design, including addressing issues like representation, accessibility, and diversity. Future game developers will need to prioritize inclusivity and consider the social impact of their creations.

7. Cross-Platform Play: Cross-platform gaming is becoming the norm, allowing players on different devices to connect and play together. Game designers will need to account for varying input methods and hardware capabilities while ensuring a fair and enjoyable experience for all players.

8. Environmental Sustainability: Game development has an environmental footprint, and there is a growing awareness of the industry's responsibility to reduce its impact. Future game studios may adopt more sustainable practices, such as using renewable energy and minimizing waste.

9. Data-Driven Design: The use of data analytics to inform game design decisions will continue to grow. Developers will rely on player data to tailor gameplay experiences, balance mechanics, and identify trends that can shape future updates.

10. Emerging Genres: New genres and gameplay experiences will emerge as technology advances. From metaverse-style experiences to innovative narrative-driven games, the possibilities are vast, and developers should be ready to explore uncharted territory.

11. Global Collaboration: With the ease of remote work and online collaboration, game development teams are becoming more diverse and international. This global collaboration can lead to unique perspectives and innovative game concepts.

12. Education and Skill Development: As the demand for skilled game developers continues to rise, the availability of educational resources and training programs will expand. Future developers will have access to a wealth of learning materials to hone their craft.

In conclusion, the future of game design and development is bright and full of exciting possibilities. Embracing emerging technologies, ethical considerations, and a commitment to inclusivity will be crucial for developers looking to make a significant impact. By staying adaptable and continually learning, you can be at the forefront of shaping the next generation of gaming experiences.

Section 20.5: Lifelong Learning and Adaptability in the Gaming Industry

In the ever-evolving landscape of the gaming industry, one of the most critical attributes for success is a commitment to lifelong learning and adaptability. This section explores the importance of these qualities and offers insights into how game developers can stay ahead in this dynamic field.

Embracing Lifelong Learning

The gaming industry is a hotbed of innovation, with new technologies, tools, and trends emerging regularly. As a result, game developers must be enthusiastic learners, continuously seeking to acquire new skills and knowledge. Here are some strategies to embrace lifelong learning:

1. *Online Courses and Tutorials:* *There are countless online courses, tutorials, and resources available on platforms like Coursera, Udemy, and YouTube. These can help developers acquire new programming languages, software, or design techniques.*

2. *Networking and Collaboration:* *Engaging with other developers and industry professionals through online forums, social media, and industry events can provide valuable insights and foster collaboration.*

3. *Open Source Contributions:* *Contributing to open source projects is a fantastic way to learn from experienced developers, gain practical experience, and give back to the community.*

4. *Read Books and Articles:* *Keeping up with industry-related books, blogs, and articles can provide fresh perspectives and keep developers informed about the latest trends and best practices.*

5. *Experimentation:* *Don't be afraid to experiment with new technologies or approaches in personal projects. Hands-on experience can be one of the most effective ways to learn.*

The Power of Adaptability

Adaptability is the ability to pivot and adjust in response to changing circumstances or requirements. In the gaming industry, where technologies and player expectations evolve rapidly, adaptability is a key factor for success. Here's how developers can cultivate adaptability:

1. *Stay Informed:* *Continuously monitor industry news and trends to anticipate shifts in technology or player preferences.*

2. *Agile Development:* *Adopt agile development practices that allow for flexibility and rapid adjustments during the development process.*

3. *Feedback Loop:* *Establish feedback loops with players and stakeholders to gather input and make iterative improvements to your games.*

4. *Cross-Training:* *Encourage team members to cross-train in different areas of game development, enabling them to fill multiple roles as needed.*

5. *Evolving Skill Set:* *Be willing to diversify your skill set. If you're primarily a programmer, consider learning about game design, art, or audio to gain a holistic perspective.*

6. *Iterate and Pivot:* *Don't be afraid to iterate on game concepts or pivot to a new direction if it improves the overall quality and marketability of your project.*

Conclusion

The gaming industry is both demanding and rewarding, offering countless opportunities for those who are willing to learn and adapt. By embracing lifelong learning and cultivating adaptability, game developers can not only thrive in this competitive field but also contribute to the innovation and growth of the industry. Remember that the journey of a game developer is an ongoing adventure, and each new skill acquired and lesson learned adds to the depth of your expertise and creativity.